101 Questi

POPES

AND THE

PAPACY

101 Questions & Answers on
POPES
AND THE
PAPACY

Christopher M. Bellitto

Paulist Press
New York/Mahwah, NJ

The Scripture quotations contained herein are from the New Revised Standard Version: Catholic Edition Copyright © 1989 and 1993, by the Division of Christian Education of the National Council of the Churches of Christ in the United States of America. Used by permission. All rights reserved.

Cover design by Cynthia Dunne
Book design by Lynn Else

Copyright © 2008 by Christopher M. Bellitto

Library of Congress Cataloging-in-Publication Data

Bellitto, Christopher M.
    101 questions & answers on popes and the papacy / Christopher M. Bellitto.
    p. cm.
    ISBN-13: 978-0-8091-4516-4 (alk. paper)
    1. Popes—Miscellanea. 2. Papacy—Miscellanea. I. Title: One hundred one questions & answers on popes and the papacy. II. Title: One hundred and one questions & answers on Popes and the papacy. III. Title.
    BX957.B45 2008
    262'.13—dc22

                                                                2007050473

Published by Paulist Press
997 Macarthur Boulevard
Mahwah, New Jersey 07430

www.paulistpress.com

Printed and bound in the
United States of America

Contents

C. The Early Modern and Modern Church (ca. 1600–today)

PART II: POWER AND SYMBOLS, CARDINALS AND CONCLAVES

C. Papal Death and Succession

D. Worldliness

Dedication

For Fr. Francis J. Corry,
who first taught me that the church had a history
and then showed me how to teach it.

"For gladly would he learn and gladly teach."
—Chaucer's Clerk, "General Prologue," *Canterbury Tales*

Acknowledgments

Kevin Carrizo di Camillo, my friend and colleague at Paulist Press, invited me to write this book during the busy papal transition period of spring of 2005, as the church mourned and buried John Paul II, then witnessed the conclave that elected Benedict XVI. From conception to birth, this book is better because of his guidance, support, advice, and insights.

As I compiled and edited the questions, too many colleagues to name commented on working lists of questions and answers. I am indebted to the wisdom, cajoling, and correction of these church historians, theologians, ecumenists, and scripture scholars who shared their thoughts based not only on hard-core scholarship, but on their experience in the classroom, the media, and public lecture halls. I would, however, like to single out Richard R. Gaillardetz, Brother Jeffrey Gros, FSC, Michael McGarry, CSP, and Gerald O'Collins, SJ, who along with members of my family read and commented on the manuscript in whole or part. I am grateful, as well, to the students, reporters, and audience members who often challenged me to clarify points. I took their comments to heart, incorporating some and deciding against others; this fact does not diminish my gratitude, but I am, of course, responsible for the final version of this material. I thank, as well, members of the talented Paulist Press production team: Manager Theresa M. Sparacio, copyeditor Dianna Walsh, and book designer Lynn Else.

Finally, and as always, I thank Karen Bellitto, my wife and my best friend, for being her and for helping me be me.

Preface

In the spring of 2005, when John Paul II passed away and Benedict XVI was elected, I was asked to write this book because of my interest in the papacy. That interest is scholarly, but one of my goals has been to spread academic research to a broader audience. Having taught the history of the papacy to seminary and state university students, I have also interacted with radio listeners, television viewers, newspaper readers, and public audiences. Particular parts of this story were shared with reporters, catechists, teachers, and general audiences, especially in parishes. The questions that ended up in this book, therefore, are frequently not mine but theirs—and maybe yours. Before we begin, a few of my own starting points should be laid out.

First, this book is neither a hall of fame nor a hall of shame. The most important recent history of the papacy includes the phrase "saints and sinners" in its title. Papal history is as much about the high points as it is about the low points. Representative popes from both of these camps are here, to be sure, but most popes fall between hero and scoundrel. I have tried throughout to name some popes who are less famous than others, but who nevertheless played a significant role in church history for better, for worse, and sometimes for both.

Second, my intention is not to produce a work of advocacy or indictment. I don't want to evangelize or scandalize, revise or attack, debunk or skewer. I have avoided using certain historical moments or phrases as proof-texts. Whitewashed history does no one any good; it is bad history because it is incomplete history.

Third, and stemming from this second point, I want to stress that this is a "both/and" book, not an "either/or" book. To use a contemporary example first: Have there been priest-pedophiles and did irresponsible bishops cover up their crimes? Yes, but the over-whelming majority—surely better than 95 percent—of bishops and priests are the good guys. Did Renaissance popes promote their children and grandchildren to cardinal, divert church money to their family bank accounts, and plot to push their enemies aside? You bet, but these are the sexy stories that conspiracy the-orists and Catholic-bashers love. Those fellows were a very small minority of popes, not the norm, but we live in an age where the criminal and immoral actions of the few disproportionately taint the praiseworthy actions of the many. To speak too much of the "good popes" risks downplaying the dark chapters of the "bad popes," but to speak only of the "bad popes" does a disservice to the far larger achievements of so many others. (I should note that I only use these phrases "good popes" and "bad popes" here—and put them between quotation marks, at that—because of a student who said I should only talk about the "good popes" and not the "bad popes," because we shouldn't air our proverbial dirty laundry in public. I replied that I talk about popes, period, and let history take care of the rest.)

Fourth, the history of Christianity is not only the history of the papacy. Were this true, we'd fall into that old "great men of history" trap. Still, we can indeed see important parts of church history through the prism of the papacy and individual popes. As the church changed, or failed to, so too did the papacy—or not. Watching how the papacy responded and adapted, or didn't, to dif-fering circumstances is a mirror through which we can understand how any institution grounded in the past must face a fluid present and unknown future. Moreover, institutions are never just institu-tions: they are groups of people trying to live and work in a par-ticular place and time. This fact is the major reason why this book's title speaks of "popes and the papacy." The men are never operat-ing in a vacuum; the institution of the papacy is staffed by flesh-and-blood believers. No pope is greater than the papacy itself.

Fifth, we begin with history. In fact, part I of this book largely proceeds chronologically. I confess to being a church historian, so this is how I see the story and how I think we can best encounter the papacy. We must begin with the history and then return to specific aspects, themes, and topics of that history that recur, which is why parts II and III of this book take a more focused approach, but only after we have seen the whole picture step by step.

The Early Papacy

		Roman emperor Constantine protects Christianity			
Death of Jesus	Peter martyred in Rome				
|	|	|			
C. 30 AD	**C. 64**	**313**	**325**	**381**	**431**
			|	|	|
			Nicaea I		Ephesus
				Constantinople	
				|	

Medieval/Reformation Papacy

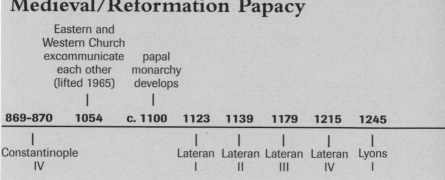

	Eastern and Western Church excommunicate each other (lifted 1965)	papal monarchy develops					
	|	|					
869–870	**1054**	**c. 1100**	**1123**	**1139**	**1179**	**1215**	**1245**
|			|	|	|	|	|
Constantinople IV			Lateran I	Lateran II	Lateran III	Lateran IV	Lyons I

Medieval/Reformation Papacy

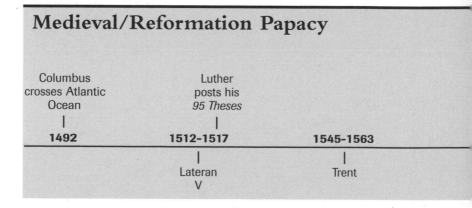

Columbus crosses Atlantic Ocean		Luther posts his *95 Theses*	
|		|	
1492		**1512–1517**	**1545–1563**
		|	|
		Lateran V	Trent

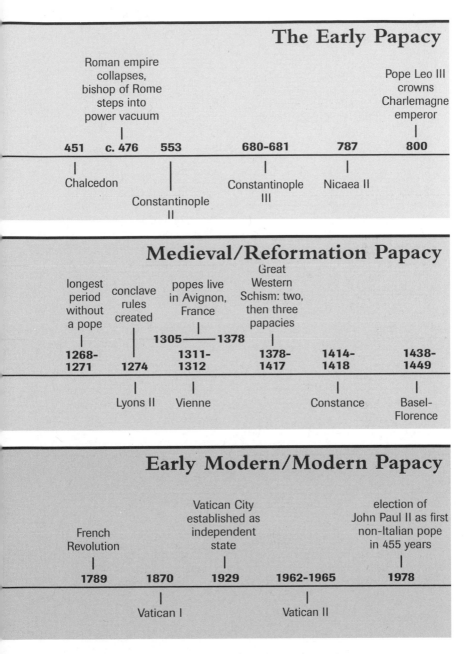

The Early Papacy

Roman empire collapses, bishop of Rome steps into power vacuum

Pope Leo III crowns Charlemagne emperor

| 451 | c. 476 | 553 | 680–681 | 787 | 800 |

Chalcedon

Constantinople II

Constantinople III

Nicaea II

Medieval/Reformation Papacy

longest period without a pope

conclave rules created

popes live in Avignon, France

Great Western Schism: two, then three papacies

1305———1378

| 1268–1271 | 1274 | 1311–1312 | 1378–1417 | 1414–1418 | 1438–1449 |

Lyons II Vienne

Constance

Basel-Florence

Early Modern/Modern Papacy

French Revolution

Vatican City established as independent state

election of John Paul II as first non-Italian pope in 455 years

| 1789 | 1870 | 1929 | 1962–1965 | 1978 |

Vatican I

Vatican II

Prologue

1. Was Peter the first pope?

Yes, but not in the way modern readers might think. Jesus selected Peter from among his twelve disciples and set him apart in a leadership position that, over the course of time, came to be called "pope," with the bureaucracy behind him eventually being called "the papacy." Peter was a first of some kind, a person set apart from the others. He is the man tradition says led the Christian community in the city of Rome—the center of the Roman Empire—and was martyred there, probably around AD 64 in a wave of persecutions under the emperor Nero. But Peter did not wear a white cassock, celebrate Mass at St. Peter's Basilica, run the Vatican, write encyclicals, or name cardinals.

Because this is a key question for history and theology, we must spend some time with the scriptural precedents for saying that Peter was the first pope. These passages will be debated, interpreted and reinterpreted, and used as foundations and criticism during much of the church's life that followed Jesus and Peter. Some will say these passages point to Peter as "the first pope"—if only in a very rudimentary way—and others will say these passages point to Peter as a kind of "first among equals," just a spokesman, a shared decision maker, or a presider among others.

Matthew 16:18–19 provides the absolutely essential moment. These verses follow a scene in which Jesus asks his followers who people say he is. Some say he is John the Baptist or a prophet, like Elijah or Jeremiah. Jesus presses his closest disciples to answer the question. Peter responds that Jesus is, indeed, the Messiah and the Son of God. Jesus praises Peter and then says: "And I tell you, you are Peter and on this rock I will build my church, and the gates of

Hades will not prevail against it. I will give you the keys of the kingdom of heaven, and whatever you bind on earth will be bound in heaven, and whatever you loose on earth will be loosed in heaven." So important are these words that a condensed form of these two verses in Latin is inscribed in huge letters in the dome above the high altar in St. Peter's Basilica.

The other critical passage that sets Peter apart is John 21:15–17. Here, the resurrected Jesus takes Peter aside and asks him three times if Peter loves him; this is after Peter denied knowing Jesus three times on the night during Holy Week now called Holy (or Maundy) Thursday. Three times Peter says yes, and Jesus tells him to feed his sheep and lambs. As this gospel paints the scene, Peter and Jesus are physically standing apart from the others. Jesus gives this special charge to Peter directly and individually.

Similarly, in the scenes in Acts of the Apostles right after Pentecost (see, for instance, chapters 2 to 4), Peter is playing a leading role and is often the first to speak up, to proclaim Jesus' resurrection, and to say that miracles are taking place in Jesus' name and not by human authority. The other disciples are present—preaching, teaching, and performing miracles—but Peter seems to have taken the lead.

2. This means that Peter was the leader after Jesus, right?

It seems so. At the same time, there are other passages in the New Testament that indicate Peter is the leader of the apostles, but not the only person selected by Jesus to spread the good news or to make binding decisions for others.

Here is one example. In John 20:19–23, it is the first evening of the Resurrection, just a few days after Jesus' crucifixion, and the disciples are hiding in fear. Though the doors are locked, the resurrected Jesus appears, shows them his wounded hands and side, and then breathes on them, saying "Peace be with you" and "Receive the Holy Spirit. If you forgive the sins of any, they are forgiven them; if you retain the sins of any, they are retained." It appears here that the authority given to Peter in Matthew 16:19 has now been given to all the disciples. In another scene that details the first Pentecost, Acts 2:1–4, a driving wind fills the room and tongues of fire appear. The fire separates into individual flames that rest on each of those present. Here again, as some later scholars and preachers would argue, the power of the Holy Spirit came not just to Peter, but to all of the disciples present.

In other moments from scripture, Peter does not appear to be acting as sole leader. For example, very early in the church's life, during the first few months and years, the question came up: "Do you have to be a Jew in order to be a follower of Jesus?" To answer this question, the leaders of this initial "Jesus community" came together in Jerusalem perhaps only fifteen or twenty years after the Resurrection, which likely took place around AD 30. At this "council of Jerusalem," as it is conventionally called (Acts 15:1–21), Paul and Barnabas stated that you did not have to be Jewish to be a Christian, while others said you had to be Jewish, which in practice meant that males had to be circumcised and everyone had to follow Jewish law, especially the food regulations we call keeping kosher. Peter seems to agree, but it is James, the leader of Jesus' followers in Jerusalem, and not Peter who announces he has come to a decision: you can be a Christian without being a Jew.

In another account of the same event, Paul's Letter to the Galatians (2:1–10), Paul distinguished his leadership from that of Peter and James. Indeed, in Galatians 2:6, Paul doesn't seem to defer to leaders in Jerusalem even though it appears he had traveled there in order to have his apostolic ministry recognized: "And from those who were supposed to be acknowledged leaders (what they actually were makes no difference to me; God shows no partiality)— those leaders contributed nothing to me." To put it generously, Paul offers a model of shared decision-making: everyone came together and collectively agreed—or agreed with Paul, as he would have it—that both Jews and Gentiles could be Christians. In the next few verses (Gal 2:11–14), Paul goes even further to relate that, on a later trip that Peter took to Antioch, Paul rebuked Peter—"I opposed him to his face"—because Peter was not following the Jerusalem agreement.

Peter and Paul continually appear together in church history, but sometimes in tension. In fact, Acts of the Apostles was originally just called Acts (to mirror a literary genre of the ancient Greek world), but the two major players are Peter and Paul. According to scripture scholar Raymond E. Brown, "Occasionally, therefore, scholars prefer the designation: Acts of Peter and Paul."[1] Some of the earliest writers in church history mention both Peter and Paul as the leaders of the Christian community in Rome. The first lists of Roman bishops, dating to about AD 160–185, designate Peter and Paul as co-founders of the church at Rome. By the middle of the third century, June 29 was set aside as the Feast of Peter and Paul in Rome, but about the same time, Peter was generally recognized as the first bishop of Rome. Face St. Peter's Basilica today and, on either side of the steps leading into the church, there is a statue of Peter on one side and Paul on the other. Many parish churches and cathedrals have an artistic representation of Peter and Paul together; June 29 remains their shared feast day.

3. Some of my Protestant friends insist that the papacy isn't found in the Bible. Is it?

The words *pope* and *papacy* (or, for that matter, *trinity* or *transubstantiation*) don't appear in the Bible, but Catholic theology allows for authentic development from roots in scripture and tradition.[2] More than a thousand years after these scriptural events—in the Middle Ages and then especially in the sixteenth century— some reformers eventually called "Protestant" will argue that the papacy was an invention or, if the papacy did have roots in Peter's relationship with Jesus, that the leadership of Peter's successors had become seriously muddled. Even Catholic reformers writing before Martin Luther in the early 1500s criticized the medieval papacy for its worldliness and power, saying that it bore little resemblance to

the poor, decentralized Christian communities that Acts of the
Apostles and the New Testament letters describe. When the Roman
Empire fell, the bishop of Rome took on many of the trappings and
administrative structures of imperial power. According to critics,
that fact doomed Peter's religious leadership to become the power-
hungry and corrupt medieval papacy that some sixteenth-century
reformers labeled with strong condemnations by calling the popes
the Antichrist, the prince of Christ's enemies, or the whore of
Babylon from the Book of Revelation.

But this is the harsh and angry side of the story. Others interpret scriptural precedents and early church history to say that leadership strayed from its roots. Yes, there was always a bishop of
Rome, starting with Peter, who held a special commission from
Jesus, but there were at the same time bishops of other Christian
communities dotting the outline of the Mediterranean Sea—
sometimes called "a Roman lake." According to this interpretation,
all of these bishops collectively shared in the decision-making
power of a decentralized model of church. Peter and his successors
in Rome enjoyed a particular prestige as a source of unity and
primacy—a technical term we will explore later—but he did not
hold any jurisdictional or legal power over any of the other bishops, either as individuals or when they gathered together in councils. So, for them, the papacy became more than what Jesus
intended when he set Peter apart.

4. Is the papacy a human institution or a divine institution?

Like the church herself, it is probably best to speak of the
papacy as a human institution of divine origin. Catholics believe
that God started the church and the papacy, but both are staffed by
human beings who are going to make mistakes. Popes of any historical period, whether they are scoundrels or saints, are never
more than human. Their failings will tarnish the papacy just as their
achievements will make it shine.

5. Is there a kind of model pope in church history?

No. Just as different periods in a country's history need different types of leaders, church history is full of a variety of popes. Some were clearly conditioned by their times—one thinks of the papal patrons of the Renaissance. Others acted in a countercultural sort of way, which often occurred in the nineteenth and twentieth centuries, with varying levels of success, because many popes did not know what to make of "modernity" in terms of helping or harming the faith. Most recently, Pope John Paul II (1978–2005) was a man who both embraced his own historical context—in the sense of using the mass media effectively as a tool for evangelization—and critiqued the times in which he lived by offering condemnations of both capitalism and communism.

We will look at these changing times and popes in part I, but an overview is in order. During the first four centuries or so of Christianity, bishops in Rome and elsewhere took a sometimes rocky road as they tried to figure out what their particular local and universal responsibilities were. A bishop, wherever he lived, was surely charged with the care of souls in his diocese, but did he have any legal and/or spiritual authority beyond his geographic borders? Did bishops of larger places—especially the five most important of Antioch, Alexandria, Constantinople, Jerusalem, and Rome—have any extra duties or jurisdiction? Was the bishop of Rome simply one bishop among others or did his special place as Peter's successor grant him an individual status? Was this status ceremonial or did it hold real authoritative power over anyone or everyone else?

The institution that came to be called the papacy changed very much when it passed from being poor and persecuted before Constantine to being favored and even imperial afterward. When the Roman Empire collapsed, there were a few shining examples of leadership (or intrusion, depending on one's perspective) in approximately the years 400 to 850. For the next several centuries, the bishop of Rome was a pawn for local Roman aristocrats before the German secular rulers boosted the pope's power. But then German authorities had to fight back the very same papal force they had helped create. The Middle Ages can be seen as both a high and low point for the papacy, which now operated as a monarchy, before Catholic and then Protestant reformers raised their voices against corruption in the half-millennium period of 1100–1600. Popes spent most of the following centuries looking inward, although many were very interested in the missions across the Atlantic and in Africa, Asia, and elsewhere. We will see the papacy challenged by the Scientific Revolution and the Enlightenment, struggling to relate to a world of rapid technological change, and responding finally to some of these changes with mixed success. Throughout, we will encounter "good" and "bad" popes, as well as see a cycle in which the very notion of the papacy changes as it goes through successive periods of challenge, consolidation, recovery, and reaction.

PART I

History[1]

A. The Early Church
(ca. 50–800)

6. Where does that word *pope* come from?

The word *pope* comes from the Greek word *papas* (father) that became the Latin *pater*. The title pope wasn't exclusively the Roman bishop's for several centuries. It was used during the first centuries of the Western, Latin church for all bishops, not just the bishop of Rome. By the fourth century, the word came to be used for the bishop of Rome alone, though the Greeks in the East continued to use it for a longer period of time for both priests and bishops. While we're at it: the word *pontiff* comes from the Latin word *pontifex* or "bridge builder" between this world and the higher world of God—or the gods. In fact, Christianity picked up the pagan word for a priest here. The leader of religious activity in the classical Roman world was an elected official called the highest or chief priest, *pontifex maximus* (even Julius Caesar held this position). This is still one of the pope's titles and, if you go to Rome and see a pope's tomb, you might see an abbreviation inscribed there: *Pont. Max.* or *P.M.*

7. Are you saying that the first one or two dozen popes weren't really "popes"?

As we said about Peter himself, we can't think of his successors for about three hundred years as popes in any medieval or modern image. For three hundred years after Jesus, Christianity was an outlawed religion in the Roman Empire. To be a Christian was to be a pagan and a traitor to Rome, because the Roman religious system placed the emperor close to—or even on par with—the gods. To worship any God other than the pantheon of Zeus and the many other gods was to go against Rome religiously, politically, and culturally. So some of the goals of the bishop of Rome were simply to survive, to lead the Christian community in the city of Rome, and to keep Christians safe during the periodic persecutions that threatened them.

The first bishops of Rome, then, were local leaders who, over time, exercised a broader regional and then "universal" leadership— bearing in mind that the Roman Empire's universe at that time essentially meant Europe, north Africa, and parts of the Middle East. The Roman bishops weren't the only bishops, though, and every other bishop was going through much of the same difficulty in spreading the faith, protecting his flock, and keeping Christianity alive. Some of those other bishops, who were also called popes in the sense of being the local father, were at times more powerful and influential than the bishop of Rome, either because they were stronger men or because their areas were intellectual—and sometimes safer—powerhouses. We think especially of the Christian communities in Alexandria, Antioch, Jerusalem, and Constantinople. These four cities, along with Rome, were the "big five" in early Christianity and their leaders came to be known as patriarchs. Eastern bishops believed the church's executive or administrative power rested among these five, though all bishops when gathered together in a council shared ultimate authority.

8. Does this mean the bishop of Rome was "first among equals"?

"First among equals" is a well-known phrase, but it complicates rather than illuminates this subject. It seems that, at the start, there were several leaders or elders in the city of Rome, as there were in almost every Christian community, although Antioch seems to have had a single bishop early on. The natural, charismatic leader among them was spokesman, chief evangelist, and central liturgical celebrant—the *papas* or father. Various words were used for these ministers: in Latin, *sacerdos* or *presbyter* (later "priest") and in Greek, *episcopos* ("inspector" or "supervisor," then later "bishop"). The bishop, in Rome and elsewhere, exercised a very basic leadership role within his community and with respect to the other Christian communities. It appears, for instance, that the head of each Christian community spoke up against persecution. When the Romans wanted to attack Christianity, one of their strategies was to critically injure the local community of believers by killing the leader, the bishop, in the hopes of scattering the followers. In Rome and elsewhere, bishops were typically the first Christians to be killed and many of them, along with their followers, became the church's first heroes as martyrs.

Each bishop was also the contact person for exchanging letters with other Christian communities and for hosting visiting bishops. Historians look at these bishops as acting something like a modern corresponding secretary writing for their community and only sometimes in their own name or with their own authority. Many bishops' letters existed throughout the Mediterranean world: to and from local bishops, sometimes including Rome and sometimes not. Over time, Rome emerged as a place through which all questions facing the scattered and sometimes-persecuted Christian communities eventually passed. So, yes, the bishop of Rome was de facto exercising a central role that not every bishop exercised, very importantly because he could trace his spiritual ancestry back to Peter, but also because in practical terms the city of Rome was the beating heart of the Roman Empire. If a bishop had a question or sought advice, it made sense to send the message to Rome because that was the spot through which most of the authority and news—secular and Christian—flowed. The church in Rome often had more experience and a broader perspective from which to draw when decisions needed to be made in order to keep all Mediterranean Christians on the same page.

But not every bishop was willing to defer to the Roman bishop. We find a certain ambivalence, in fact: Rome was recognized as special because of Peter and Paul, but challenges to Rome were not uncommon. Some writers took the "rock" of Matthew 16:18 to mean the church or the body of the faithful in general and not just Peter (and his successors) individually. They said the rock was the faith itself and "on this rock" referred to all of the disciples, not just Peter. Origen, a Greek theologian ca. 185–253, wrote that the rock is "every imitator of Christ from whom they drank, who drank from a spiritual rock that followed them." For Origen, the keys of the kingdom were given to all who agreed with Peter that Christ was the Messiah and repented for their sins, as Peter had done.[2] (In part II of this book, we will explore in greater detail the challenge of north African bishops to Roman authority in order to examine later discussions of whether the bishop of Rome's primacy—or "first-ness"—gave him a legal supremacy, as well.)

9. How did bishops of Rome respond to some of these challenges?

Bishops of Rome often invoked the fact that they could trace their ancestry and authority back to Peter. This is known as *apostolic succession,* and the bishops of all the leading dioceses similarly traced their power back to the first apostles and then down through their successors. (Every bishop today is called a successor to the apostles.) But it all comes back to first principles: because Peter was seen as having that special and unique commission from Jesus, the argument also follows that Rome's authority trumped those of other bishops because they were descended not from Peter but from the other apostles. Only the bishop of Rome stood in Peter's place.

Callistus I (ca. 217–222) was among the first bishops of Rome to invoke Peter's authority explicitly. Stephen I (254–257) used the phrase *cathedra Petri* (chair of Peter). More than just bishops of Rome backed Peter's sole authority, too, especially if they were in the western part of the Roman Empire. A bishop named Irenaeus of Lyons (in Roman Gaul, which is modern-day France), who died around the turn of the third century, and a theologian named

Tertullian (ca. 160–220) interpreted Matthew 16:18 to mean that Jesus gave Peter both a first place and a supreme power. This power reached the whole church and was held by the other bishops, but it flowed through Peter and his successors as bishops of Rome, making Roman apostolic succession the most important line of all.[3] Jerome (ca. 347–419), the famous translator of the Bible from Hebrew and Greek into the Latin Vulgate version, also supported this claim. He wrote to Damasus I, the bishop of Rome (366–84) who had commissioned his translating, "It is to the successor of the fisherman that I address myself...As I follow no leader save Christ, so I communicate with none save Your Beatitude, that is, with the chair of Peter. For this, I know, is the rock on which the church is built."[4]

By the middle of the fourth century, bishops of Rome were asserting that any decisions made by Christian communities outside Rome had to be submitted to Rome before they could be considered valid and binding for everyone. Julius I (337–52), for instance, was angry that bishops who gathered in Antioch in 341 did not inform him that they had condemned the views of Athanasius of Alexandria, even though his understanding of Jesus' divinity corresponded to the creed that came out of the church's first general council, held at Nicaea in 325, which Athanasius had attended. Though Nicaea had clearly taught Jesus' divinity, the next decades still saw great confusion about orthodox belief. Julius took the opportunity not only to defend the church's belief that Jesus is "one in being with the Father," but used the debate to assert his own place as the final arbiter of dogma (doctrinal statements of belief) and discipline (including who was a legitimate bishop). As Julius wrote forcefully to the bishops at Antioch: "And why were we not written to about the church of Alexandria in particular? Do you not realize that it has been the custom for word to be sent to us first, that in this way just decisions may be arrived at from this place [Rome]?" Lest the bishops think that Julius was simply another bishop and equal to them, Julius added, "I am informing you of the tradition handed down from the blessed apostle Peter."[5]

Two years later, a regional council in Sardica agreed, which was very important: it was one thing for the bishop of Rome to assert his authority, but quite another for other bishops to recognize that claim. At Sardica, the bishops agreed to "honor the memory of the apostle Peter and provide that letters be sent to Julius, bishop of Rome." In addition, they decided that when a bishop was accused of a crime or heresy, the ultimate judge would not be his fellow bishops, but the bishop of Rome. Innocent I (401–417), was pleased to receive from some bishops of north Africa a letter asking him to approve their actions against heretics. Innocent told them: "Nothing which was done even in the most remote and distant provinces should be taken as finally settled unless it came to the notice of this See [the diocese of Rome], that any just pronouncements might be confirmed by all the authority of this See, and that the other churches might from thence gather what they should teach."[6]

10. I know that the Roman Emperor Constantine became a believing Christian. What was the Donation of Constantine?

In the early fourth century, the Roman Emperor Constantine favored Christianity and protected it from persecution. He endowed the church with money, perhaps with land in central Italy that would become the papal states (see question 83), and certainly with buildings in the city of Rome. For later critics of the papacy, this Donation of Constantine, as it came to be known, was the beginning of the end of the early church's purity. According to this interpretation, when Christianity and her first bishops, including the bishop of Rome, were poor, they were pure. An imperial papacy, following this line of thought, was essentially invented by Constantine, who took the authentic but local leadership of the bishop of Rome and inappropriately ratcheted it up several degrees.

You also may have heard that the Donation of Constantine was proved to be a forgery. This is partially true: in 1440, an Italian humanist named Lorenzo Valla demonstrated that the manuscript called the Donation of Constantine was a forgery dating to the 700s. Critics of the wealthy medieval popes used Valla's analysis to assert that the bishops of Rome were not, in fact, legitimate in their use of temporal or worldly power in addition to spiritual authority. While it is true that the piece of paper was surely written about 400 years after Constantine, it's hard to question the historical record that the emperor did indeed protect the church and provide her with land, money, and privileges. (It would be like really being married, but finding that your marriage certificate was fake: you are still married, but the piece of paper isn't valid.) Now, it can be legitimately argued that Constantine's gifts were the first step in a slippery slope toward papal worldliness, greed, and raw power, but the historical fact remains: for better or for worse, when the Roman Empire collapsed, the bishop of Rome was in a position to take charge because Christianity was now protected and playing a leading role in religious and political matters.

11. This arrangement sounds like a two-edged sword. Was it?

Having lots of money, land, and property is not always a blessing. With such things come responsibilities that can be distracting. For example, Leo I (440–461) cared for the safety and material needs of the Roman population, Christian and otherwise, by negotiating with the Huns and Vandals to spare the city of Rome. Likewise, Gregory I (590–604) took office while Rome was suffering from a plague and food shortages; moreover, the bishop of Rome's lands, dating back to Constantine's endowment, were mismanaged. Gregory reorganized the administration of his churches and property, redistributed money to the poor and starving, and set up systems for debt relief, food, and shelter. In doing this, he was building on the organization of the city of Rome and its suburbs into seven regions that had been done centuries before by Fabian, bishop of Rome (236–50), one of the church's martyrs during the persecution of the pagan emperor Decius. Gregory didn't mind addressing the needs of his people; indeed, he is the first pope to call himself "servant of the servants of God." But he did complain in a letter that he sometimes felt he was nothing more than a paymaster, because he was even in charge of treaties, public safety, and the upkeep of a military force that had to defend Italy from invasion because there was no longer a Roman emperor or Senate to do so. Still, Gregory was able to balance these civil duties with religious ones. He saw beyond the Italian peninsula by enthusiastically sponsoring missionaries all the way up to England. His two most important works were spiritual writings: a handbook for parish priests and a series of model sermons based on the Old Testament book of Job that emphasized virtue and exhorted Christians to act in a morally responsible way.

Not every pope who followed was as good a man and pastor as he was: few could multitask like Gregory the Great. And there can be no denying that secular duties, even if taken up reluctantly and with an admirable sense of responsibility, did pull some popes further away from their spiritual obligations. There is a reason for that cliché that power corrupts and absolute power corrupts absolutely.

So, one side of the two-edged sword is that the spiritual leader, the bishop of Rome now called pope, was mixed up with temporal power. The other side of the two-edged sword is that civil leaders saw themselves as religious leaders also, and sometimes even thought they were higher than bishops and popes. Once again, the situation started with Constantine, who defined himself as the defender of the Christian faith, sometimes going so far as to depict himself as a thirteenth disciple, a priest, *pontifex,* and a brother to the bishops. On his coins, Constantine wore emblems of Christianity and in his letters often referred to himself as having been placed by God as the church's protector.[7] This iconography of power, if we can call it that, certainly foreshadows what became the "divine right of kingship" theory: a certain family ruled because God wanted them to rule—at least according to that family's interpretation.

12. When the Roman Empire fell, why didn't the power of the bishop of Rome fade away, too?

Shortly after tolerating and then beginning to favor Christianity in the early fourth century, Constantine built a new capital that he named after himself: Constantinople, now Istanbul in Turkey. The empire was just too large to administer from Rome at this point, so he established a second court in Constantinople. This arrangement allowed the bishop of Rome to grow in power, even though there was always a pair of co-emperors (one in Rome and one in Constantinople). For many reasons, the capital in Constantinople fared better than the capital in Rome, making the emperor in Constantinople gradually more powerful. In fact, the eastern emperors will claim to keep the Roman Empire alive until 1453, when Constantinople fell to the Turks.

Back in Rome, the bishops stepped into the power vacuum left by the western emperor and empire. They adopted much of the imperial machinery: the Latin language, the system of administrative *dioceses* (a Roman imperial word), architecture (a *basilica* is a Roman receiving hall), the way of handling correspondence, the formulas for writing law (called a *decretal*), and some of the court ritual, as well. Although the western empire was fading, the power of the bishop of Rome did not because of a series of strong popes who asserted the power of Peter within church affairs and who exercised strong leadership in temporal matters because no one else was around to do so.

13. Which bishops of Rome stepped into the power vacuum?

There are a fair number of strong bishops at this point, some of whom we've already met (Leo I, Gregory I) and many of whom were very much men of the late Roman Empire. Because they'd been trained as civil administrators—the typical job for a bright young man—these men took that imperial style and bureaucratic mind-set with them into their new roles as bishop of Rome. In the late fourth century, before Leo I and Gregory I, Damasus I and Siricius (384–99) took steps toward centralizing Rome's authority over against that of the local bishops. Damasus I heard appeals of local bishops over the heads of their metropolitans (the bishops of the largest dioceses in a region). He set himself up as a judge of local councils' agreements, disagreements, and decisions. By directing his secretary Jerome to translate the Bible into Latin, Damasus I established Peter's successor as the authority on biblical interpretation and authenticity. Siricius made more direct interventions into diocesan affairs. He dealt with bishops in Gaul and Spain as if they were his subordinates; he sent instructions without waiting for appeals or requests for advice; and he wrote in the royal "we" to say that "we decided" on a certain matter, "we issued" a particular ruling, and "we prohibited" this idea or action.

14. How did the popes justify their authority?

These popes relied on their role as Peter's successor to assert their authority over other bishops. Concerned that the bishop of Constantinople, the second most important city in the Roman Empire, would compete with him, Damasus I noted that Rome's primacy came from Christ through Peter; he was also the first bishop of Rome to use the word *apostolic* with special reference to Rome. Leo I was the first to use that old pagan Roman title of *pontifex maximus*. He engineered a decree of the Emperor Valentinian III in 455, which declared that any bishop refusing the bishop of Rome's summons to the city must be forced to come to Rome by the civil provincial governor. Ten years before, Valentinian had decreed that "whatsoever the authority of the apostolic see has sanctioned, or shall sanction, let that be held as law for all."[8]

Within the church, Leo I helped establish doctrine: his letter, called a *Tome,* was a major source for the teaching on Jesus issued by the Council of Chalcedon (451). At the council, bishops even shouted, "Peter has spoken through Leo!"[9] But Leo incurred the anger of many eastern, Greek bishops when he later unilaterally rejected one of the council's statements that placed the bishops of

Rome and Constantinople on equal footing while acknowledging that Constantinople held second place after Rome. For these bishops, the matter had been settled because together they had made a decision at a council, which was the final church authority in their eyes. For Leo, the matter was not settled unless and until he said so, because Peter was the prince of the apostles and, in turn, the pope was prince of the successors of the apostles, the bishops. In his sermons and letters, Leo promoted the idea that Peter was still at work in his successors, saying "Peter especially rules all whom Christ also ruled originally," and that, "even in our own time…[papal power] is to be ascribed to [Peter's] work and his guidance." Some bishops did not argue: the bishop of Ravenna forwarded a question from another bishop onto Rome, "since blessed Peter who lives and presides in his own see, offers the truth of the faith to those who ask." Leo also noted that, while each bishop is a successor to the apostles, each has a responsibility for his area alone and only partially shares universal authority, while only Peter's successor is fully responsible for all Christians everywhere.[10]

15. It sounds like the popes were now saying their power was not only over the other bishops, but over the emperors, too. Is this where the idea of "church and state" comes from?

If you took someone from the first fifteen hundred years of Christianity, dropped him into the modern world, and then tried to explain the separation of church and state, he would have two reactions. First, he wouldn't know what you were talking about. Then, once she understood it, she'd think you were crazy. Civilizations predating Christianity and then following for a millennium and a half after Jesus took for granted that religion, politics, and culture naturally went together; they were all, to use a common expression, one and the same.

This unity works nicely, of course, until a pope or bishop and a king or emperor wonders whose power is ultimately higher. If

Constantine is protecting a Christianity only recently made legal, what's the harm? But what happens when a later emperor sins? Here's that two-edged sword again. In fact, conflict came a little more than fifty years after Constantine's conversion. An emperor named Theodosius was blamed for a massacre and, in 390, Ambrose, the bishop of Milan, excommunicated the emperor. Theodosius was readmitted to communion only after he did public penance. Ambrose took the opportunity to lay down an important precedent: bishops judge Christian emperors and not the other way around. "Where matters of faith are concerned it is the custom for bishops to judge Christian emperors, not for emperors to judge bishops." For Ambrose, no one, not even the emperor, is above the law, especially church law. As he told Theodosius, "The emperor is within the church, not above the church."[11]

About a century later, a bishop of Rome named Gelasius I (492–96) established what became known as the Gelasian doctrine or "two swords" theory in a letter to the eastern emperor Anastasius. Gelasius I held that one sword represented spiritual power and the other sword temporal power. God gave both swords to Peter and his successors. The spiritual authority delegated temporal power to a ruler, like a king or emperor, who was therefore the spiritual authority's inferior. "Of these," Gelasius I wrote, "the responsibility of priests is more weighty insofar as they will answer for the kings of men themselves at the divine judgment. You know, most clement son, that, although you take precedence over all mankind in dignity, nevertheless you piously bow the neck to those who have charge of divine affairs and seek from them the means of your salvation."[12] At the end of time, the church argued, the spiritual ruler would have to give an account for the actions of all the souls in his charge, including the souls of kings and emperors. On earth, then, the spiritual authority had to guide the temporal power to keep his soul safe from damnation. As a way of emphasizing this, references to the emperor as *pontifex* or *sacerdos* were discontinued; popes called emperors, and other bishops also, "sons" and not "brothers."

Ambrose and Gelasius I were building on precedents. Two Jewish models come from first-century BC Pharisee texts called the *Testament of Judah* and the *Testament of Naphtali*. The first states, "As the heaven is higher than the earth, so is the priesthood of God higher than the earthly kingdom"; the second says, "Levi [priestly class] laid hold of the sun and Judah [royal class] seized the moon." (The sun outshines the moon because the moon has no light of its own, but only reflects the sun's.) The New Testament was also a basis: 1 Corinthians 2:15 declares that the spiritual man will be judged by no one. Over time, this spiritual man came to be identified with the pope, who could not be judged by his fellow bishops, a general council, or any civil official. This came to be translated into Latin: *papa a nemine iudicatur*—the pope may be judged by no one—and found its way into the most important medieval collection of canon law. Gratian's twelfth-century *Decretum* stated that the pope judges all and may be judged by no one unless he deviates from the faith— that is, becomes a heretic—in which case he ceases ipso facto to be pope. Left unresolved is the obvious question: Who decides that the pope has deviated from the faith? A good question, and one to which we'll return when we talk more about church councils.

16. How did the emperors and kings respond?

It was often a delicate and awkward dance that sometimes got ugly and out of step. One pope's idea of imperial interference can be one emperor's idea of legitimate protection of the faith. At first, when the emperors and popes were in agreement, there wasn't much trouble. With Constantine, the state protected the church and then, when Rome fell, church and state were merged into one—just as paganism and the Roman Empire had naturally gone together. We have seen that Ambrose and Gelasius I asserted fairly quickly that when there is a dispute, there is no question that the spiritual authority tops royal power. Within a few centuries after the fall of Rome, however, a new power emerged, this time in northern and central Europe, which would put the Gelasian doctrine to the test.

In the 700s, the bishops of Rome needed physical protection. A man in the north named Pepin the Short, who had great power but no crown, asked Pope Zacharias (741–52) to decide who should be king. Zacharias ruled that Pepin should be king because he had the actual power even if his claim to the throne was not as strong as others'. Zacharias was pleased to be consulted, as this put Pepin in his debt and seemed to acknowledge the Gelasian doctrine. Pepin was delighted to be anointed by the pope's representative; in a largely illiterate world, rituals were very important, so it looked as if the royal anointing was something like the ordination of a priest or bishop—or at least kings liked to think of it that way. For several decades, Pepin and his descendants protected Zacharias and his successors by driving out invaders and then "giving" central Italy to the popes in a Donation of Pepin that mirrored the Donation of Constantine. In turn, the popes legitimated their authority by anointing them, culminating in the coronation of Charlemagne (768–814) in Rome on Christmas Day 800 by Pope Leo III (795–816).

After this day, Charlemagne and his successors styled themselves Holy Roman emperors and heirs of Constantine as defenders of the faith. This was the key to legitimating their actions in church affairs. Charlemagne declared that his capital at Aachen was a new Rome. His seal featured Constantine's imperial titles and the Latin words for "renewal of the Roman Empire." His empire was to be a city of God and he took for himself titles that recalled Constantine and could potentially challenge papal power: vicar of Christ, vicar of Peter, rector of the Christian people, rector of true religion, priest and king, and the thirteenth apostle. By this time, there was a sense that kingship was sacred and a type of political theology had grown up justifying royal involvement in church affairs.

Although Charlemagne's grandchildren allowed his empire to collapse, a series of German kings and emperors named Otto and Henry continued the idea of protecting the church in the tenth and eleventh centuries. When a succession of very subpar men were chosen pope by Roman families who treated the seat of

Peter as their private treasure chest, these German authorities fulfilled their role as heirs of Constantine and Charlemagne to act as defenders of the faith—in this case, it seems, defending the leaders of the faith from themselves. They interceded by vetoing these papal choices, which were nothing like the secret and often independent conclave elections of the later Middle Ages and beyond. Not surprisingly, these emperors frequently engineered the election of Germans.

As a result, German emperors and Roman aristocrats battled over Peter's successor in the two hundred years bracketing the turn of the millennium in 1000. As a leading papal historian, Eamon Duffy, calculated: "Of the twenty-five popes between 955 and 1057, thirteen were appointed by the local aristocracy, while the other twelve were appointed (and no fewer than five dismissed) by the German emperors."[13] As Duffy notes, many of these reforming popes adopted the names of their formidable predecessors to signal they wanted to recover the papal strengths of a better time, so we find Clement, Sylvester, Damasus, Leo, Gregory, Victor, and Nicholas reappearing as papal names. The irony is that many of the popes who were put in place by the German imperial power turned right around and asserted the church's freedom to name her own abbots, bishops, and popes with no interference from secular authority, even though that is just how they themselves came to Peter's throne.

B. The Medieval and Reformation Church (ca. 800–1600)

17. I had a teacher once say that the papacy really got started in the Middle Ages. Is this true?

We've already had bishops of Rome and popes for a millennium by this time—that can't be denied. But it's fair to say yes to this question if what you have in mind is not only an administrative bureaucracy—what we mean today when we say "the Vatican" —but the very idea of the papacy as an abstract concept. The word *papacy* itself, from the Latin *papatus*, doesn't appear much until the eleventh century. Think of the phrase, "The king is dead. Long live the king." It doesn't seem to make much sense (or to be very tasteful or sensitive, frankly). But it reminds us that any position—a royal throne or the papal seat—is more than the person holding the job at any one time. When a president dies in office, the presidency lives on. So, too, even without a living pope, the papacy never dies.

The idea of this *papatus* was built on two movements that had been emerging during Christianity's first millennium but accelerated during the Middle Ages. The first movement is a growing administrative structure. In order for the popes to compete with monarchs and to be recognized not only as a king or emperor's equal, but his superior, they needed to mirror certain structures for administering a far-flung faith: a court (the college of cardinals), a legal system (canon law and courts to decide cases), a system of ambassadors or legates (increasingly the cardinals, but any cleric could be delegated to speak in the pope's name), a chancery to handle documentation and letters, and all the other elements that make for effective government. The second movement is more ideological: the notion of the pope as Peter, boosted by a growing "cult" (in the sense of an object of veneration) for Peter, his feast day (June 29, shared with Paul), donations sent to Rome ("Peter's Pence"), and images of him in sculpture and painting, most especially receiving the keys of the kingdom from Jesus.

Popes had to be careful, however, to emphasize that their power extended beyond Rome, which was so closely tied to Peter and his martyrdom there. In the eleventh and twelfth centuries, popes referred to themselves as the vicar of Peter *(vicarius Petri)*. As the Middle Ages progressed and royal power challenged the pope's authority to interfere (as kings and emperors saw papal appointments and actions) in their territories, the popes took to calling themselves the vicar of Christ *(vicarius Christi)*, although Gelasius I might have used the phrase many centuries earlier. This title is not only more familiar to modern ears, but one that popes took away from rulers following Charlemagne, who had been using it to describe their own semi-holy power and authority as defenders of the faith in the line of Constantine.[14]

So the Middle Ages certainly was a period of papal transformation, largely under the impetus and ideas of Gregory VII (1073–85), who even before he was selected pope had been part of the brain trust behind many of the reforming popes who preceded him. Gregory VII was an Italian named Hildebrand who spent much of his life in Rome. Because his influence and ideas were felt before, during, and after his papacy, all popes of this period are often called "Gregorian"; like Gregory VII, they were trying to make the papacy as free from outside control as possible by establishing the papacy as an independent and even supreme monarchy. These popes transformed the papacy so much that, while older textbooks call this period the Gregorian Reform, the most recent scholarship more accurately labels this medieval papacy as the Gregorian Revolution.[15]

18. I remember hearing about *investiture*. What was that and is it connected to this papal revolution?

Investiture is a word that often gives a title to these battles between a king or emperor and a bishop or pope; textbooks refer to the "Investiture Controversy" or "lay investiture." On the most basic level, it refers to the handing over or investing of a bishop or abbot with the symbols of his religious authority. Typically, these would be a miter (the pointed hat), a crosier (the shepherd's staff or crook), and a ring. Because medieval bishops and abbots frequently were also large landowners, they might also receive secular symbols, such as a clod of earth to show their ownership of land, a scepter, and a sword.

Who gave them these symbols? The person doing the investing was a superior. Sometimes this superior was religious (a bishop,
archbishop, cardinal, or papal legate), but sometimes it was a secular leader (local lord, king, or emperor). We should remember that
investiture took place in an elaborate ritual before an audience of
people who were largely illiterate. In this visual and oral culture,
what you saw and what you heard was what you knew. It must
have been very confusing, therefore, for lay people to see a bishop
or abbot kneel before a secular lord or king, receive the symbols of
power and, in central Europe, hear that secular leader say to the
clergyman: "Accept the church!"

This issue of investiture, then, is closely related to the two-
swords question: who was the higher power on earth? In more
practical terms: Who owned and ran a local parish? On the highest level: Who owned, ran, or oversaw the most important cities,
such as York, Cologne, Paris, Barcelona, Prague, or Venice? In the
countryside in Germany, especially, there was a tradition that whoever built a parish or church ran it. So the local secular lord built a
chapel, hired and fired priests whom he considered his vassals or
serfs, paid them, and took his share of the money from the collection basket. You can imagine that priests, abbots, and bishops would
not likely criticize their patrons and that, on the highest levels, the
system easily led to kings thinking the church was simply a department of their royal machinery. It was even easier to control the
church if the local lord or king just appointed a relative—son,
brother, brother-in-law, or cousin—who would owe his position,
prestige, and income to the king. Not surprisingly, these appointees
often knew nothing about theology or being moral pastors or
shepherds, which led to a decline in the church's ability to keep her
sacraments authentic, her teachings orthodox, and her operations
independent. The papacy's efforts to name church leaders might
look like a play for power and money, which admittedly it sometimes was, but that effort also had deep theological and sacramen-
tal roots and goals.

19. When popes started to choose bishops, was that a good thing or a bad thing?

Both. By naming bishops, the popes were asserting their right to be independent of the local secular power structure.[16] The ability of popes to name bishops meant that, at least theoretically, they could appoint men who were trained in theology and had experience as pastors and administrators. The system of naming bishops unilaterally was as open to abuse, bribery, and patronage by popes as it was by secular lords, of course, but this does not mean that well-meaning popes did not appoint capable bishops at least some of the time. On other occasions, however, popes named a loyal man to be bishop of a region, even though the new bishop had never been to the area or couldn't speak the local language. In these situations, loyalty (and regrettably, the heavy fees that sometimes changed hands in the papal curia) was clearly more important than suitability as far as the pope and new bishop were concerned, which often left the local clergy and laity without a sensitive spiritual leader. So the process of local clergy and informed laypeople naming their own bishops—like monks and nuns electing their own abbots and abbesses, which had been the norm for many centuries before lay investiture had become a problem—is not something to be feared. The problem was that the popes were trying to do something good—free the church—but at times they pursued that goal with a heavy-handed effort that ignored the local church.

20. So can we say that the popes were claiming some kind of "superpower"?

What they were doing was fully asserting many of the ideas and precedents of the first millennium in a comprehensive effort to apply the Gelasian doctrine and establish that, ultimately, spiritual authority was the highest power on earth. The popes wouldn't call this a superpower, though the kings and emperors probably would—but only because they wanted such power for themselves, typically. An illustrative way to explore the papal attempt at ultimate authority is to dedicate a few minutes to the correspondence with bishops and royalty found in the archives of Gregory VII (1073–85).[17] It includes a tantalizing document called the "Dictate of the Pope" *(Dictatus papae),* which is an agenda of twenty-seven topics or propositions, perhaps a table of contents for a book that was never written. Although it appears in the collection of letters from an early year of Gregory's papacy, the list could date back to 1059 when Hildebrand (not yet pope) and his colleagues might have been preparing a list of papal powers they would make the emperors acknowledge before they were crowned in Rome.[18] Some of the twenty-seven propositions deal with internal church matters: only the pope can lay claim to the unique title "universal"; only he can depose, reinstate, or transfer bishops; his legate, no matter what clerical rank, can preside and decide over the heads of bishops in council; synods, books, or laws may not be considered authoritative without his approval; his court is the highest appeal, but no one can judge him; and, using that powerful image of himself as Peter's heir, "the Roman Pontiff, if he shall have been canonically ordained, is undoubtedly made holy by the merits of blessed Peter."

Gregory VII grounded his actions in a forceful invocation of the binding authority of Peter's see. Each situation for this feisty pope became a referendum on papal influence; he often painted opposition as the sin of disobedience—a potent way to sober foes. For instance, Gregory chastised Archbishop Siegfried of Mainz, referring to him as "Your Cleverness" with a bite, for passing judgment on the bishops of Prague and Olmütz when papal authority should have prevailed. Similarly, he ordered King Haakon of Denmark "by apostolic authority" to cease slandering priests. In other letters, Gregory does not disguise his threats, warning that he will "unsheath the sword of apostolic wrath" and proclaiming "he is guilty of idolatry who refuses to obey the Apostolic See." He was not blind to crimes within the church, too, telling the people of Constance to ignore their bishop, who was guilty of buying and selling church offices, and absolving them of obedience to him.[19]

Gregory also continually made Gelasian statements, asserting that the papacy could rightly oversee territories—he laid particular claim to Spain, Hungary, and Corsica, for example—and ordered that a count who had a bishop assaulted be set upon by another bishop "with weapons both carnal and spiritual."[20] One proposition from the Dictate that strikes most people as over the top is the ninth: "all princes should kiss the feet of the pope alone." The Dictate also declares that the pope can wear imperial insignia, depose emperors, and release subjects from their oaths of fealty if the superiors, which must have included emperors, were found to be "unjust men." In practice, this meant that the pope was claiming veto power over kings and emperors: the pope could make a moral judgment on the worth of a royal person's character.

As you can imagine, an emperor was not going to take claims like these lightly. The Holy Roman Emperor Henry III (1039–56) had been quite an example of a defender of the faith. Back in 1046, he'd come to Rome, kicked out rival popes, and started the chain of events that led to the German reforming popes mentioned in question 16. His son Henry IV (1056–1105) continued what he considered to be legitimate oversight of the church, including naming and investing bishops, and saw Gregory VII as a rival. Gregory naturally resisted, starting a 1075 letter to Henry IV with a significant withholding of his blessing: "Gregory...to King Henry, greeting and the apostolic benediction—but with the understanding that he obeys the Apostolic See as becomes a Christian king." He reminded Henry that when he spoke to Gregory, he really spoke to Peter and invoked the scriptural scenes of Matthew 16:18–19 (giving of the keys) and John 21:15–17 ("Feed my sheep."). Henry was not frightened. He wrote back in words that recalled the semi-holy status of emperors like Constantine and Charlemagne as defenders of the faith and turned a few tables on the pope: "Henry, King not by usurpation, but by the pious ordination of God, to Hildebrand, now not Pope, but false monk....Our Lord, Jesus Christ, has called us to kingship, but has not called you to the priesthood....I am to be judged by God alone....Relinquish the Apostolic See which you have arrogated....Descend! Descend!" (To get a sense of the insult, imagine the Soviet leader Mikhail Gorbachev writing in the 1980s to John Paul II, but calling him by his given name "Karol," declaring he wasn't really pope, and telling him to get out of Rome.) In turn, Gregory deposed Henry in the name of Peter and released his subjects from their oath of allegiance.[21] Although there was a measure of reconciliation when Henry repented before Gregory in a Hollywood scene by standing in the snow outside a castle in Canossa, Gregory ended his life in exile from Rome after Henry's troops chased him from the city. It seemed that raw power had triumphed over spiritual theory.

21. I always hear negative things about the popes in the Middle Ages. Did they do anything good?

The expression "if you can't beat 'em, join 'em" is modern, but these medieval popes would have been comfortable with it to describe their goals. The Latin phrase to describe what the church sought was *libertas ecclesiae*—the freedom or liberty of the church. It became something of a rallying cry or slogan and it's hard to argue with the point of a papal monarchy, which was to make the church less subservient to temporal power. The church needed to be able to name her own leaders, to make her decisions freely, and to operate without oversight or interference.

We might turn to yet another letter of Gregory VII to illustrate the point. In a long letter to the bishop of Metz, Gregory carefully explained the precedents for his actions against Henry, invoking scripture, Ambrose's excommunication of Theodosius, the Gelasian doctrine, and Pope Zacharias' role in establishing Pepin as a legitimate ruler. From the beginning, there is a sense of a church under attack: "You ask us to fortify you against the madness of those who babble with accursed tongues about the authority of the Holy Apostolic See not being able to excommunicate King Henry as one who despises the law of Christ." A bit later, Gregory directly addressed the issue of supreme authority: "Is not a sovereignty invented by men of this world who were ignorant of God subject to that which the providence of Almighty God established for his own glory and graciously bestowed upon the world?... Does anyone doubt that the priests of Christ are to be considered as fathers and masters of kings and princes and of all believers?"[22]

One might fairly ask, then, what could the popes have done otherwise? To indict the popes for creating a monarchy is to misunderstand the context in which the medieval papacy lived. They frequently acted like kings, it is true, but they usually did so to fight kings as equals or superiors so the church wouldn't be under the thumb of royal power. In fact, the papacy generally succeeded—perhaps too well, in that money flowed readily into Rome—in liberating and organizing the church on the local, regional, and European-wide level.

To achieve these goals, the cardinals elected canon lawyers more than spiritual men, which is not to say the medieval popes didn't care about prayer and being priests, but that they were selected to meet the challenges of the times. Because temporal monarchies were building bureaucracies, the church also needed administrators to meet the royal powers on their own terms. There had to be a coordinated and uniform system of canon law with a clear line of appeal up to Rome. Because the church is about both doctrine (theology) and discipline (canon law), the popes supported the growth of centers of theology and legal research that became universities and, in turn, training grounds for clerics who would serve the church's bureaucracy on the local, regional, and papal levels. These places of learning—for theology and law, but later for many other fields—became the foundations for the modern educational systems of college, graduate, and professional schools in both religious and secular arenas.

Because the popes had been controlled by the local Italian families and then the German emperors, the papacy needed to transform itself into an institution outside of national boundaries and required men who could look beyond the Italian-German nexus of power. Papal representatives called *legates* (something like

an ambassador) exported the idea of the papacy as the ultimate
authority in the church and over secular governments. In turn,
these papal legates brought local concerns and ideas back to Rome.
In fact, fifteen of the nineteen popes between 1073 and 1216 had
been papal legates.[23] A career in religious and secular diplomacy, it
seems, had become the best education for a medieval pope, given
the agenda he inherited.

The major reform goal of the period—*libertas ecclesiae,* the
freedom and independence of the church—was largely a success
thanks to these medieval popes. It was no small feat.

22. But were there any downsides to these developments?

Absolutely. It's fair to say that the medieval papacy's strengths
and achievements were simultaneously its weaknesses and stumbles. As a result of the central attention many popes of this period
paid to temporal matters and politics, worldliness, ambition, and
greed crept into the papacy. In extracting itself from its cozy relationship with royalty and aristocracy, it is fair to say that the papacy
sometimes became just another monarchy when it lost track of its
special character of holiness.

For example, nearly every piece of paper or legal case that
traveled through the papal court required a fee at every level, from
the parish to the diocese to the papal curia itself. Opportunities for
bribery abound in any system full of flawed human beings, however divine the institutional church's origins are. Canon lawyer
popes helped the church defend herself, but at times at a spiritual
cost because some of these popes were more prelates than pastors.
The wealthier and more corrupt the papacy became, the more it
lost its moral authority, although we must remember that in the
Middle Ages, with a largely illiterate society with no mass communication, probably better than 95 percent of Christians had no clue
who the pope was, anyway.

23. Did anyone inside or outside the church complain about the popes becoming like monarchs at the time?

Naturally, kings and emperors complained repeatedly that the papacy was interfering in temporal matters where it had no business, at least according to the secular powers who were rejecting the two-swords theory and relying on the heritage of Constantine, Charlemagne, and the German reforming emperors. What's more interesting, however, is the criticism leveled within the church, because it demonstrates that one can love and criticize the church at the same time.

We encounter again the opposition of bishops, especially the ones of major dioceses in the Greek-speaking eastern parts of the fallen Roman Empire, to the idea that the bishop of Rome held a higher power than other bishops. This opposition had been building for centuries, dating back most clearly to Pope Leo I's refusal to accept a canon of the Council of Chalcedon in 451 that put Constantinople second in line after Rome. Periodically, clashes over authority, theology, policies like mandatory priestly celibacy, and liturgical differences occurred during the church's history, capped by the regrettable moment in 1054 when Rome and Constantinople excommunicated each other in what became known as the Great Schism.[24] (This mutual excommunication was lifted by Pope Paul VI and Ecumenical Patriarch Athenagoras I in 1965.)

During the Middle Ages, public debates and letters illustrated the challenge and critique of papal monarchy from the East. In 1112, an Orthodox lay rhetorician named Nicetas Seides debated the archbishop of Milan, telling him:

> Rome has appropriated to herself, dear brother, the monarchy which is not contained in her office and which had divided the bishops and churches of east and west since the partition of the empire....How shall we accept from her decrees that have been issued without

consulting us and even without our knowledge? If the Roman pontiff, seated on the lofty throne of his glory, wishes to thunder at us, and, so to speak, hurl his mandates at us from on high, and if he wishes to judge us and even rule us and our churches, not by taking counsel with us but at his own arbitrary pleasure, what kind of brotherhood, or even what kind of parenthood can this be?…We should be the slaves, not the sons, of such a church, and the Roman see would be not the pious mother of sons but a hard and imperious mistress of slaves.

About a century later, in 1199 or 1200, the Orthodox patriarch of Constantinople, John X Camaterus, wrote a letter to Pope Innocent III that summarizes the issue of the difference between papal primacy and supremacy for the East.

We declare that Peter was set by Christ before the other disciples, and in honor precedes the others and was exalted by such primacy. Although we believe the Church of Rome is first in rank and honor, as among sisters of equal honor, among the other Churches of God honored with patriarchal rank [the five sees were Rome, Constantinople, Antioch, Alexandria, and Jerusalem], at no time whatsoever have we been taught that she is their mother or is comprehensive of them. Such primacy and honor have been allotted to her over the years not because Peter was made bishop in Rome by Christ (surely this is not a tradition supported or handed down by Scripture) or because he died there….Such honor has been granted to your Church because at the time it was exalted by an emperor and senate, neither of which is found there any longer.[25]

24. What about when the popes were in France somewhere?

There was a period of almost seventy years, 1309–77, when the papacy resided in the southern French city of Avignon, which became a lavish administrative center. The story begins with a statement by Pope Boniface VIII (1294–1303) that is either the high point or low point of the papal monarchy, depending on your perspective. Boniface had been locked in a battle with the French King Philip IV (1285–1314, also called "the Fair" or "Philippe le Bel") over who was the highest religious authority in France. Philip had taxed the French clergy without asking the pope's permission, which violated protocol. Naturally, the pope objected and several years of posturing followed: if the king could not collect the taxes, then he would prevent Rome's money from leaving his country, too. A battle over naming a new bishop followed and when Boniface called all of France's bishops to Rome for a synod, only half went. Enraged now at both the king and some of his own bishops, Boniface issued *Unam sanctam* in 1302, which reiterated the two-swords theory, wielded many of the scriptural citations traditionally used to assert Peter's authority, and forcefully concluded "that is altogether necessary to salvation for every human creature to be subject to the Roman Pontiff."[26] Philip saw this as nothing other than a pretension of power and sent his men after Boniface, then at an Italian city called Anagni, where the French forces verbally insulted and physically intimidated the pope, who died shortly afterward from the shocking treatment.

Philip took this chance to bring the papacy, not just the French bishops, more directly under his power. An Italian pope, Benedict XI, reigned briefly but died in the summer of 1304. After nearly a year without a pope, the deadlocked cardinals went outside their own circle and chose a weak French archbishop who took the name Clement V (1305–14). He almost entirely capitulated to French power: Clement V cancelled all of Boniface's decrees against Philip, absolved the Anagni attackers, and even praised the king's zeal for the church.

A few years into his reign, Clement V moved the Roman curia to Avignon, although we should add that there were good reasons to leave Italy, which was very unstable at the time. Factional wars, especially in the areas near Rome, between papal and imperial forces made the Italian peninsula a dangerous place. Holy Roman emperors came down from Germany twice and took over the city of Rome in 1311 and 1328. So what was supposed to be a temporary stay at Avignon became long term, in no small part because the college of cardinals grew ever more French. Of the 133 cardinals created between 1305 and 1377, nearly 85 percent (112) were French, compared to just fourteen Italians, six Spaniards, and one Englishman. Avignon was also more physically attractive, with an elaborate papal palace, lush villas for the cardinals, and what we would call a comfortable standard of living for career curialists. (To understand the attraction, compare a beach or country house with the center of any city in mid-August.)

The growth of an elaborate administrative bureaucracy, already well underway as part of the Gregorian Revolution, exploded in the fourteenth century. Once established, it was hard to move the entrenched and comfortable curia and all of the administrative personnel connected to it from Avignon back to Rome. Unfortunately, this bureaucracy often translated into much corruption, with the papacy claiming all sorts of "papal reservations," meaning that only the popes could appoint officials at nearly every level of the church hierarchy. Job seekers crowded Avignon and disputes about who should get what office led to immense paperwork, legal affairs, and bribery. When offices weren't filled, the papacy claimed the right to any funds that were supposed to go to them, which offered an incentive to keeping bishoprics empty. Much of this money went not to charity, but to building residences, offices, and fortifications in Avignon. In turn, this meant that the spiritual needs of the Christian people in many places were simply ignored.

It is not surprising that the Italian humanist Petrarch called Avignon the whore of Babylon and labeled these years the "Babylonian Captivity of the Church." Recent scholarship has provided a more balanced view, while not overlooking the undeniable corruption of the Avignon years.[27] The seven Avignon popes (all French, as we would expect) were not always the dregs of the curia. A few reformers sought to improve the Dominicans, Benedictines, and Hospitallers; to support education and rigorously examine candidates for ordination as priests and bishops; to fight heresy; to resist a slavish dependence on France; and to reduce absenteeism (bishops living outside their dioceses), pluralism (priests and bishops holding more than one church office), and nepotism (getting jobs for family members), though some Avignon popes promoted these abuses because they kept the money flowing into the papal curia.

Other reformers sensed that the papacy was losing its credibility and "international" (to use the word anachronistically) prestige. Bridget of Sweden (1303–73) and Catherine of Siena (1347–80) helped to successfully call the papacy back to Rome, where it belonged, and away from Avignon, which had no connection whatsoever with Peter. Catherine, especially, was not afraid to write baldly to the pope (as she did in this letter about 1375) to declare that he should avoid nepotism and worldliness.

> I want to see you a forceful man, fearless and without earthly love for yourself or for any being related to you by blood....Thus my soul's desire, in inestimable love, is that God in his infinite mercy strip you of all [worldly] passion and all indifference of the heart and make another man of you—that is, a man re-formed in fiery and most ardent desire. In no other way can you fulfill God's will and his servants' desires....

Catherine went so far as to hint that the pope might not be worthy to be pope if he did not do as God, speaking through her, instructed:

> He demands that you do away with the enormous number of iniquities committed by those who are pastured and fed in the garden of the holy church.... Since he has given you authority and you have accepted it, you must use your virtue and your power. If you are not willing to use them, you should have refused what you took on....[28]

25. I heard that there was a time when there were several popes simultaneously. Is this what an antipope is?

An antipope is a challenger or pretender to the papal throne. There have been many: to match the more than 260 authentic successors to Peter, there have been at least three dozen acknowledged antipopes—meaning that they offered a serious challenge with a fair number of supporters, both religious (including cardinals) and secular. (I say "acknowledged" to distinguish from the many lunatic fringe elements throughout history who proclaimed themselves the true remnant of the church and one of their own as the authentic pope. The Internet has made finding these modern-day "antipapacies" easier.) The largest batch of antipopes existed during the Gregorian Revolution, when emperors and kings continued to claim their right to name the bishop of Rome against the cardinals' choice. From 1058 to 1181, for example, there were seventeen popes and fourteen antipopes. Alexander III (1159–81) alone was challenged by four men throughout his reign.

There was a period when there were two and then three popes simultaneously and no one really knew who was in charge. This confusing time lasted almost forty years and is known as the Great Western Schism. (This is not the Great Schism, which usually means the East-West split dating formally to 1054; see question 23.) It began when Gregory XI (1370–78), a Frenchman who believed strongly that Rome was the right place for the pope, moved the papacy back to Rome, but died soon afterward. The election that followed was one of the most rambunctious ever. The Romans, who had been without their bishop for three-quarters of a century and whose economy suffered considerably, rioted several times. But the April 1378 conclave of sixteen cardinals was deadlocked between Frenchmen who wanted to go home and Italians ready to stay in Rome. When another riot threatened the conclave, the cardinals faked the election of an 80-year-old Italian cardinal, stood him in a window to placate the crowd, and ran away to the Castel Sant'Angelo, where they compromised on an Italian archbishop (the last non-cardinal ever elected pope) who had spent his career in Avignon.

Urban VI (1378–89) had serious psychological problems: he called one cardinal a half-wit, struck another, and picked fights with everyone. A few months later, the cardinals decided that they had made a mistake in the April conclave. They claimed their election was invalid because they had been afraid of the Roman mob during the voting, so they held another conclave.[29] This time, they selected a French cardinal who became Clement VII (1378–94). Each pope excommunicated the other, made his own college of cardinals, and enjoyed some military support in a few small skirmishes. In time, Clement VII naturally returned to Avignon and the church was split in two, with religious orders, dioceses, and countries taking sides. Imagine how confusing it must have been for the people of Toledo in Spain to go to Mass and hear a prayer: for the true pope, whoever he is.

For the next three decades, whenever a pope from Rome or Avignon died, the other side claimed a conclave could not legitimately be held because their man was the only true pope. Neither side recognized the other and various efforts for a compromise (such as mutual abdication) fell apart, at one point because of fears of assassination. Finally, in 1409, a majority of cardinals from both sides stepped in, decided that the church as the seamless garment of Christ could not be divided this way, and held a council at Pisa, where they declared the Roman and Avignon popes deposed. Then they elected one of their own as Pope Alexander V (1409–10). But neither the Roman nor the Avignon pope considered the Pisan council to be legitimate because he hadn't called it, so they simply ignored the cardinals' action and this Pisan or conciliar pope, as he came to be known. As a result, from 1378 to 1409 there were two popes and two colleges of cardinals; after 1409, there were three.

26. Three popes at once! How did they figure that one out?

Good question. The church had a millennium of history that said the pope may be judged by no one, dating back to 1 Corinthians 2:15 and extending through the Gelasian doctrine and many other papal statements, landing finally in medieval canon law, which admitted that a pope who became a heretic would stop being pope. Trouble was: Who could make such a decision? Around these questions there arose a theory, rooted in church history and canon law, called conciliarism.[30] It asserted that, in certain—and usually only very extreme—circumstances, a general council could judge and even depose a pope, particularly if he was guilty of heresy or schism. Conciliarism was a diverse set of ideas, not one universally accepted principle, that ranged from those who believed a general council is always the highest authority in the church to others who said the college of cardinals was a kind of aristocratic elite who should take over the church in the case of a heretical or schismatic pope. Some wanted a general council to meet regularly, such as once every decade, while others said councils should only meet in dire situations. Was the pope the highest authority or not? If the church was not a monarchy but more of a corporate body, maybe the pope was a delegated minister, like a modern prime minister or president, who could be recalled in a vote of "no confidence" or through an impeachment trial.[31]

The Great Western Schism, with its two and then three popes, provided conciliarists with their best chance of applying their ideas. Certainly, the situation was dire and extreme, but the council of Pisa had clearly failed to resolve the schism. Nevertheless, the Pisan/conciliar Pope John XXIII (1410–15), who had followed Alexander V, called the Council of Constance (1414–18) because he was sure he would be elected (or reelected) since he had the Holy Roman Emperor's support.[32] When it became clear, however, that none of the three contending popes could be elected or reelected because this would only continue someone's claim, John XXIII fled Constance at night, figuring the council would simply fall apart. What happened was just the opposite.

The Council of Constance was one of the most impressive gatherings of the church's best and brightest in history (second only, perhaps, to Vatican II, 1962–65), but it was also one of the most dangerous moments in the church's life. Constance's leaders, composed of representatives from all three sides, as well as a large number of people who had become neutral in disgust, knew that if they failed there could be permanent division in the church. They systematically explained their actions based on precedent, theology, and canon law, noting that this situation of three papacies seemed to be an extreme and never-to-be-repeated situation. Their strongest expression of conciliar authority came in a document called *Haec sancta synodus,* issued a few weeks after John XXIII's departure. It declared that the council was "lawfully assembled in the Holy Spirit" and that "it holds power directly from Christ; and that everyone of whatever estate or dignity he be, even papal, is obliged to obey it...."[33] The council deposed the Pisan/conciliar Pope John XXIII, who eventually renounced his papal claim and was reconciled to the church, and the Avignon Pope Benedict XIII, who neither attended nor sent representatives and never accepted Constance's legitimacy or actions. Benedict XIII held onto his claim until his death in 1423. The Roman Pope Gregory

XII decided to abdicate, but first he had his representative declare the council officially opened in his name. This meant that the council's later actions, including the papal election, would be legal and binding.

Still afraid that any conclave might be split three ways, the council decided that, for this time only, the conclave would be expanded and the vote carefully regulated. In addition to the total of twenty-three cardinals from the three rival colleges, thirty representatives of the council (five delegates from each of six national groupings) would also vote in the papal election. The successful candidate would have to receive a two-thirds majority from each of the three groups of cardinals plus two-thirds from each of the six national groups, which would insure widespread support and no dissident wing. Remarkably, after thirty-nine years of schism, the conclave took just three days to elect Martin V (1417–31), a cardinal who was loyal to the Roman line of popes.

27. Did this Council of Constance prove that a council is higher than the pope?

Here's the tricky part. Before Constance, the medieval popes had successfully used general councils as well as smaller synods on the local and regional levels to institute their policies and spread the notion of papal monarchy. There had been dozens of such meetings throughout Europe in the Middle Ages, capped by seven general councils. Four of these (Lateran I in 1123, Lateran II in 1139, Lateran III in 1179, and Lateran IV in 1215) were held on the pope's home turf in Rome, marking the city once more as the epicenter of Christianity. The councils of the first millennium had witnessed more imperial control and collaborative decision-making, but the papacy had come to dominate the general councils in the Middle Ages.

At Constance, on the other hand, conciliarism had stepped in to solve the Great Western Schism, which no pope had been able to do for almost four decades. It certainly appeared that a corporate or constitutional body had trumped a monarchy. Certainly, too, the papacy had been damaged by the abuses in Avignon and the very long schism. Some scholars and theologians hold that Constance proved that a general council is the highest authority in the church.[34] The papacy naturally came down on the other side: the schism and Constance's conclave were remarkable, unique, and one-time-only events. The relationship between popes and councils was rocky, at least in the decades after Constance, but the papacy recovered fairly strongly in the rest of the fifteenth century, only to be met with new challenges led by Martin Luther and John Calvin in the sixteenth century.

28. How did the popes fight back against the conciliar folks?

We can look at the next few decades of the fifteenth century as a papal restoration, a process that will be repeated in the next century after the Protestant Reformation. Martin V pursued an agenda of reestablishing the papacy as the official voice and authority of Christianity. To pursue this goal, he reorganized the curia; worked against secular and conciliar challenges; increased income from the papal states, which had been interrupted and confused for over a century because of the Avignon papacy and Great Western Schism; signed private treaties with different nations; overhauled the church's taxation system; and named bishops. His underlying point was that these were activities that only a pope, not a general council, could perform.

Martin V was succeeded by Eugene IV (1431–47), who was no friend of general councils either, but who called one at Basel because he was following the stipulations of Constance, indicating that conciliarism was still strong enough that it couldn't entirely be disregarded. This council became a last stand of the staunchest conciliarists, who believed the pope was nothing more than a delegated minister, against Pope Eugene IV and the strongest proponents of papalism. Eugene was so angered with Basel's attempts to circumscribe his leadership that he ordered the council dissolved, but he was forced to back down when his own legate refused to proclaim the decree and resigned. Eugene seized the initiative by moving the council to Italian territory, first to Ferrara and then Florence, because it would be easier to meet with representatives of the Greek East. Eugene's plan was to engineer a union of East and West, thereby proving that he was the ultimate authority in the church. An accord was signed in 1439, but it was a dead letter almost immediately when eastern bishops soon disagreed over theological aspects of the agreement. Still, Eugene had demonstrated that he was the man to speak to when decisions had to be made for the church. He continued to press this point by unilaterally signing concords with other Christians, including the Armenians, Copts, Syrians, Chaldeans, and Maronites.

Meanwhile, a competing council continued to meet at Basel. The delegates there invoked *Haec sancta synodus* from Constance, declared that popes had to call general councils, and said popes must be reminded of this fact each year when they celebrated the anniversary of their election. Eugene, in turn, said that the delegates remaining in Basel were "a faction of agitators" meeting in a false or rump gathering "without any authority," and taking sacrilegious actions. He then excommunicated them, but they kept meeting, declared Eugene deposed, and elected in his place a layman as Felix V (the last acknowledged antipope).[35] Conciliarism's moment had passed, however, and Felix V later "resigned" and was reconciled with Pope Nicholas V (1447–55), who had succeeded Eugene IV. The last few Basel holdouts then "elected" Nicholas and adjourned. The deathblow, at least on paper, came when Pope Pius II (1458–64), ironically a former conciliarist himself, issued a statement declaring that any remaining conciliarists were "imbued with a spirit of rebellion," guilty of spreading a "deadly poison," and holding positions that were "erroneous and abominable."[36] Under strong papal influence, another general council, Lateran V in 1516, reiterated that only the pope has the power to call, transfer, and dissolve a general council.

29. I know that Martin Luther comes along at some point and says that the papacy is the Antichrist. Why did he say this?

We should begin by acknowledging the Renaissance papacy as one of the low points in church history in terms of the quality of men sitting on Peter's throne. Caricatures of popes from wealthy families—the Medici, the Borgias, and others—with mistresses, children, and grandchildren are based in hard fact and incontrovertible evidence. It is something of a rogues' gallery, led by Sixtus IV (1471–84), Alexander VI (1492–1503), Julius II (1503–13), and Leo X (1513–21), who famously—or infamously—said that if God saw fit to make him pope, the least he could do was enjoy it. All of them, plus popes before and after, followed the Italian practice of patronage. Church offices were bought and sold constantly; it was the norm. Popes made their children and grandchildren, some of them only teenagers, into bishops and cardinals; they spent great amounts of money patronizing humanists, artists, architects, and sculptors. Many of their efforts at adorning Rome and commissioning scenes from the life of Christ, especially those depicting Peter's authority, were part of the continuing papal restoration after the Avignon papacy, the Great Western Schism, and the conciliar challenge.

The proverbial straw that broke the camel's back for Martin Luther (1483–1546), an Augustinian monk and scripture professor in Germany who set out to be a reformer, not a revolutionary, was the selling of indulgences where the money would be sent to Rome to build a new St. Peter's Basilica, which is the one still standing there today. Some of the money was also earmarked to pay off the bribes and debts incurred by a German archbishop who bought three dioceses, making him guilty of simony (the buying and selling of church offices) and absenteeism, because he could only be in one place at a time. Luther's *95 Theses* were nothing other than talking points, many of them very fair and objective criticisms, meant to bring together a critical mass of discussion for reform efforts. The strong papal reaction against him and his ideas,

however, quickly turned his pen sharper and he attacked the
papacy repeatedly for the next thirty years.[37]

In a short pamphlet from 1520 titled *An Appeal to the Christian
Nobility of the German Nation,* Luther sought to tear down what he
called three walls in Christianity: the first was the notion that the
church had secular power, the second was the pope's ultimate
authority when it came to interpreting scripture, and the third was
the idea that only a pope could call a council. At one point when
writing about scriptural interpretation, Luther asked rhetorically,
"Has not the pope made many errors?...[I]t is plain enough that
the keys were not given to St. Peter only, but to the whole
Christian community." To Luther, the problem was clear: the
church needed reform and a council was the best way to accom-
plish this goal. But the pope himself was resisting, which made
Luther conclude: "[I]f the pope should exercise his authority to
prevent a free council, and so hinder the reform of the church, we
ought to pay no regard to him and his authority."[38]

It wasn't long before the papacy was being attacked as the
whore of Babylon and Antichrist itself by Luther and especially by
those who followed him, who were often far angrier and more virulent than he was (at least at the start of his career). Woodcuts and
pamphlets, now cheap and available in the early sixteenth century
since Gutenberg had perfected the printing press a few decades
earlier, offered visual images that contrasted Jesus with Antichrist.
The most well known and damaging at the time was the German
Passional Christi und Antichristi, produced in 1521 by a friend and
sympathizer of Luther's. Other images soon followed, although
Luther was not the first and certainly not the last to make the connection between the papacy and Antichrist.[39]

These attacks on the papacy led to a strong and continuing
distrust of papal leadership in every area of European life, not just
religious but also political. Secular leaders had long been battling
popes for supremacy. The prior two centuries had not been the
strongest for the papacy, despite the recovery from conciliarism, and
the Renaissance papacy seemingly did everything it could to dis-

tance itself from the poverty and purity of the gospels. Luther's challenge had another consequence, therefore: it gave political leaders the chance to build on precedents (Constantine, Charlemagne, and the Ottos and Henrys as defenders of the faith, for example, or more recently Philip the Fair's successful controlling of the popes) and try to finally take over the church in their lands.

30. Is this where England's Henry VIII as "Head of the Church of England" comes in?

Yes. Henry VIII (1509–47) was really not much of a Protestant in terms of his theology. What he wanted to be was pope in his own country, and toward this goal he was building on precedent. William I (1066–87, "the Conqueror") had asserted certain unwritten ancient customs: no bishop or abbot could recognize the pope until the king did; all papal letters must be shown to the king before promulgation, insuring a veto of papal policy and decisions; no papal legate could enter the kingdom without royal approval; and no religious official from England could go to Rome without the king's permission. William I had even sent a letter to Gregory VII, the architect of papal monarchy himself, refusing Gregory's demand that the king perform a rite of fealty to him. Henry VIII's 1534 *Act of Supremacy* basically went a step further: he simply replaced the pope with himself as chief religious leader in England by saying the monarch had no superior monarch, even if he was the pope. His daughter Elizabeth I, during her long reign of 1558–1603, reiterated the English monarch as "Head of the Church of England" in 1559 and decreed the *Thirty-Nine Articles* that firmly established Anglicanism as Protestant in 1563, stating clearly that the pope held no jurisdiction in England.

31. What was the Catholics' response?

As you can expect, the popes saw Henry VIII and Elizabeth I in England, along with the Protestant reformers in Europe, as heretics who had denied the sacraments, Catholic theology, the traditions of church authority, and especially the very idea of the papacy. But we should remember that, before and at the same time as Luther, other reformers who remained Catholic had been criticizing the papacy not because they wanted to tear it down, but because they were trying to build it back up. They felt the popes themselves were most guilty of staining Peter's throne and authority. It must be admitted, because it simply cannot be denied, that many of the critics, inside and outside the church, were right about the papacy. Many of the papacy's problems were its own doing, even if they had started with admirable goals such as the freedom of the church to name her own officials. But wholesale reform couldn't follow Luther immediately, even in the eyes of cardinals and popes who were wise and humble enough to see the trouble, because to change the papacy would be to admit wrongdoing and tell the world the critics were right.

We should mention, however, that a few popes weren't afraid to admit Rome's internal problems even after Luther's *95 Theses* started what became a tornado of protest. Pope Hadrian VI (1522–23), a Dutchman who was the last non-Italian pope for 455 years before Pope John Paul II's election in 1978, admitted, "We know that for many years many abominable things have occurred in this holy see....No wonder the illness has spread from the head to the members, from the supreme pontiffs to the prelates below them. All of us (that is, prelates and clergy), each one of us have strayed from our paths; nor for a long time has anyone done good; no, not even one."[40] Pope Paul III (1534–49), aware that a corrupt curia was unlikely to patrol itself, called reformers from outside Rome into the city and ordered them to write a frank assessment of the situation. Their memo on reform directly said the problem started with simony at the church's highest level, the papacy, and trickled down like poison from Rome. The city of Rome should be an example of goodness for others, but instead, "all strangers are scandalized when they enter the basilica of St. Peter where priests, some of whom are vile, ignorant, and clothed in robes and vest-

ments which they cannot decently wear in poor churches, celebrate Mass. This is a great scandal to everyone."[41]

Finally, the Council of Trent, which met in stages over a long
period of time (1545–48, 1551–52, 1562–63), responded directly
(as if Luther's excommunication wasn't direct enough) by reassert-
ing the church's hierarchy as well as by producing helpful teachings
on the canon of scripture, the nature of justification, and the sacraments. In the years after Trent, the papacy sponsored missions to
the New World being explored and conquered after Columbus'
first voyage in 1492; in 1622, Gregory XV (1621–23) set up the
Congregation for the Propagation of the Faith. More importantly
for our story, the papacy turned inward by exercising its authority
over the church's body. Shortly after the council, Pius IV
(1559–65) reserved to the pope, sitting over a group of designated
cardinals, the right to decide on conflicting interpretations of
Trent's decrees and implementation. Successive popes then issued a
Roman catechism, profession of faith, breviary (the cleric's book of
daily prayers), missal (containing the service for Mass), and revised
Latin Bible. Pius V (1566–72) strengthened the Inquisition and the
Index of Forbidden Books to monitor orthodoxy and hunt for
heretics. Sixtus V (1585–90) reorganized the curia and ran the lines
of authority more directly to and from himself rather than through
committees of cardinals.

Other popes, reacting to the Protestant challenge that the
papacy was an invention, continued the medieval and Renaissance
practice of adorning Rome and reminding people of Peter's presence there. St. Peter's Basilica was completed and then extended
under Paul V (1605–21). The Italian architect Gianlorenzo Bernini
(1598–1680) added the distinctive semicircle of columns that
reaches out from the church's doors to embrace St. Peter's Piazza,
while also crowning the high altar inside with an elaborate canopy
and adding a shrine to St. Peter's chair behind it.

The Renaissance effort at papal centralization was as focused
as the medieval popes had hoped it would be. As far as the popes
were concerned, they were once again at the center of Christianity

and sitting at the top of the hierarchy. What they needed was a voice to make their claims known again outside Rome. That voice came from a Jesuit, Cardinal Robert Bellarmine (1542–1621), who defended the papacy as strongly as possible.

32. How could this cardinal, Robert Bellarmine, defend the papacy after all that had happened over the last two centuries?

There were many heated exchanges called "controversies" between Catholics and Protestants in the contentious climate of the sixteenth and seventeenth centuries. These public debates, played out verbally and in writing, were the talk-radio programs of their day. Catholic and Protestant universities had professors who specialized in such "we're-right-you're-wrong" literature. The Jesuit theologian and cardinal Robert Bellarmine was responding to a particular attack on papal authority. He confronted the continuing question, dating back to the first millennium's two-swords theory, of who was the higher power: the pope or the king/emperor. Bellarmine's answer, put in the mouth of a fictional pope, could easily have been written more than a thousand years before by Ambrose or Gelasius I, or 500 years earlier by Gregory VII.

I am the pastor appointed by Christ, who is the Lord of all the flock. You, the people, are the little sheep; your kings are the rams. As long as your kings continue to be rams, I permit them to rule and lead you. But if they turn into wolves, will it be right that I permit the sheep of my Lord to be led by wolves?...Christian people ought to obey a lawful king, one who does not turn you from the law of God and the Catholic religion and who is therefore loved by me, the vicar of Christ, as a son. Obey him in those matters, not when he orders what is against the law of God and the Catholic faith. But a king who tries to turn you aside either by allurements or by other means from the path that leads to life, and who has by my sentence been cast out from association with the pious and deprived of his realm, you will not consider a king....[I]f through the keys of Peter that king should be declared a heretic and excommunicated and deposed, it then will not be a sin not to obey him.[42]

It does seem striking that after the considerable papal failures and embarrassments of Avignon, the Great Western Schism, the conciliar challenge, and the many critics of the papacy from nearly every spot along the ideological spectrum, voices were raised in support not only of the pope's authority over Catholicism, but even his power above that of secular leaders. Still, one way of fighting back when attacked is to stand your ground and refuse to change course, even when that very course is the source of the greatest criticism.

33. I keep hearing that the popes started a "siege mentality" after the Reformation. What does this mean?

This notion of a "siege mentality" needs a chronological tune-up. In our own past half-century, the phrase was invoked to talk about a church that retreated from a dangerous world to hide behind walls. Pope John XXIII (1958–63) was essentially attacking this approach with Vatican II, which was supposed to open the Vatican's windows to let the dusty, stale air out and the fresh, clean air in. This dramatic image led some to pit the Council of Trent against Vatican II, saying that Trent was closed and dark while Vatican II was open and bright—clichés for both councils that should be tossed aside.[43] But it is true that scholars struggled to define the papacy after the Protestant Reformation and Trent. Some use the phrase "Catholic Reformation" to indicate a certain open-minded approach among critics and reformers both before and after Luther; others prefer "Counter-Reformation" because it connotes a more defensive, even revenge-minded papacy fighting back against Protestants to reestablish authority and cast out enemies.[44]

The papacy in the century after Trent was indeed powerful and focused on making itself the unchallenged head of the church once more, but there were other, more innovative forces at work, too.[45] Only over time, when the church and papacy faced one challenge after another to the very idea of faith and monarchy (as with the Scientific Revolution and the Enlightenment, which we will explore shortly), did the popes really shore up the walls and turn almost entirely within, especially after the French Revolution decimated the church in France and Napoleon took not just one, but two popes prisoner. Certainly, by the end of the early modern age in the middle of the nineteenth century, a siege mentality was well established.

C. The Early Modern and Modern Church (ca. 1600–today)

34. What were some of the achievements of the popes in this period?

Popes of the seventeenth, eighteenth, and nineteenth centuries frequently spent more time on secular affairs than religious matters, sometimes for good reason.[46] This period witnessed a more remote papacy than the intimate pastoral relationship offered by John XXIII or John Paul II at the end of the twentieth century. Like the medieval papal monarchs, post-Reformation and early modern popes were mostly administrators, career curialists, aristocrats, and diplomats. Of the twenty-nine who reigned between 1540 and 1770, just about 10 percent were theologians while nearly two-thirds were canon lawyers.[47] Some of these popes resisted innovation to hang onto their political status quo even though that kind of power was dwindling steadily; others took a leading role in the recovery of a vibrant spirituality, scholarship, and especially evangelization through missionary activities and sponsorship of religious orders devoted to spreading Catholicism in the Americas, Asia, and Africa. It pays to spend a few moments with some of these achievements in order to moderate, though we cannot entirely balance, the political entanglements of the papacy in this long period between Luther's age and our own. We can look especially at the end of the nineteenth and beginning of the twentieth century for some of these achievements.

First, a movement that came to be called social Catholicism or Catholic social teaching received a great boost from Pope Leo XIII (1878–1903). He was an aristocrat, but he nevertheless kept an eye out for the castoffs of the Industrial Revolution, who were suffering in the slums produced by a brutal and impersonal factory system long before child labor laws and just wages were legislated to protect workers. Think of any Charles Dickens novel or story you may have read. *Oliver Twist* certainly comes to mind. *A Christmas Carol* is not a sentimental holiday story, but a ripping indictment of the capitalist Scrooge who cares nothing for his overworked employee Bob Cratchit and his impoverished family. With an encyclical called *Rerum novarum* in 1891, Leo XIII placed the church on the side of the workers, pressing owners to treat employees with justice and fairness. Leo stressed that the family and not the state was the building block of any society; it should be protected, particularly by the common bond of religion. His support for unions caused them to flourish, leading not only to trade organizations, but to service movements like Catholic Action in Europe and Dorothy Day's Catholic Worker movement, which began in New York City in 1933 and spread during the Great Depression. So important was this movement to protect workers' rights that a number of popes followed *Rerum Novarum* with their own encyclicals updating the topic: Pius XI's *Quadragesimo Anno* on its fortieth anniversary (1931), John XXIII's *Mater et Magistra* on its seventieth (1961), and John Paul II's *Laborem Exercens* on its ninetieth (1981).

Second, we again look to Leo XIII, this time for leadership in scholarship. He opened up the Vatican's Secret Archives to scholars regardless of their faith, invigorated a rediscovery of the great debt the church owed to the medieval scholastic theologian Thomas Aquinas with the encyclical *Aeterni Patris* in 1879, and encouraged Catholic scholars to pursue modern methods in church history, archaeology, the natural and hard sciences, theology and philosophy, and scripture study. More than anyone else in the Middle Ages, Aquinas had worked to reconcile faith and reason, inspired by the famous medieval statement that predated him: *credo ut intelligam*—"I believe so that I may understand." In 1998, Pope John Paul II, himself a heavyweight intellectual with two doctorates, also discussed this faith-reason balance in *Fides et Ratio,* in which he frequently cited *Aeterni Patris* and Aquinas.

Third, we find papal leadership in getting the people in the pews to read the Bible. In 1757, Pope Benedict XIV allowed people to read the Bible in their own vernacular language as long as the translation had been approved in Rome. Soon translations, sometimes with the common language in one column and the Latin in an adjoining column, appeared in Italian, Spanish, and Portuguese. Within fifty years of Benedict XIV's action, more than seventy translations of the Bible had been published.[48] Leo XIII started the Biblical Commission, laid the groundwork for the Pontifical Biblical Institute, and removed the prohibition that prevented laypeople from reading parts of the Mass in their own native language instead of Latin, which few people knew anyway. Pius XII in 1943 wrote a very influential encyclical called *Divino Afflante Spiritu* that recognized the achievements in scriptural analysis that had flourished in the past century. Pius XII encouraged scripture scholars to employ modern methods to interpret the text for meaning and historical context, to avoid fundamentalism, and to distinguish among different types of literature in the Bible.

Finally, a grassroots movement for eucharistic devotion and active participation in the liturgy was boosted by Pius X (1903–14), who wanted people to sing, to appreciate Gregorian chant, and to participate actively in the Mass instead of just watching it go by. Pius X encouraged Catholics to receive the Eucharist often, even every day, which was a radical departure from the widespread practice of receiving only two or three times a year. Pius X paved the way for frequent reception of communion by saying a person could receive if he or she wanted to do God's will and had not committed a mortal sin, which mitigated the norm of no communion without immediate confession beforehand. He moved the age for First Communion to about seven, down from the teenage years, as well. Pius XII (1939–58) allowed some vernacular rites, commissioned a new translation of the psalms, made it even easier to receive communion, oversaw the renewal of Holy Week, permitted a vernacular version of the epistle and gospel to be read after it was proclaimed in Latin, and then let laymen be lectors for the vernacular reading. Under John XXIII (1958–63) and Paul VI (1963–78), Vatican II's document on the liturgy *Sacrosanctum concilium* and the later instructions that followed it opened up the Mass and Bible study all the more.

35. Did a pope really condemn Galileo for saying the earth revolves around the sun?

I knew we'd get to this one. The answer is yes—kind of. The thing to remember is that the issue was less about astronomy and science than authority. The pope in question was a complex man, Urban VIII (1623–44): a very well-educated aristocrat, humanist, diplomat, patron of artists and architects (including Bernini), and generous supporter of missions and evangelization, but also a pope guilty of nepotism, greed, absolutist tendencies, and poor political decisions. Some scholars think of him as the last Renaissance pope in the best and worst senses. Like some of his predecessors, Urban VIII was fascinated by astronomy and supported scientists in their work, including his friend Galileo (1564–1642), whom he had praised in print and defended from condemnation while still a cardinal.

As long as Galileo asserted that the idea of the earth revolving around the sun was an experiment or hypothesis, he was left alone. He had been warned to do so by none other than the papal defender Robert Bellarmine. With the election of his friend as Pope Urban VIII, Galileo felt comfortable in going further to state as scientific fact the Copernican or heliocentric model of the sun as the center of the solar system. When Galileo did so, he ran into trouble because it conflicted with the church notion of the earth as the center of the universe. We must remember that the ultimate interpreter of the Bible was the pope and he would not give up this authority, especially only a century after the Protestants had said everyone could read and interpret the Bible for themselves. Galileo must have been surprised (if not shocked and even betrayed) to find that his former defender, now Urban VIII, had moved the conversation from astronomy, mathematics, and science to theology, authority, and obedience. In 1633, Galileo was faced with condemnation and chose to take back his scientific statements; he spent the rest of his life under house arrest and was unable to teach or write publicly.

To jump a few centuries ahead: the rehabilitation of Galileo was one of the earliest tasks John Paul II explored, starting just a year after his election. The pontifical commission he ordered to reopen the case concluded in 1992 that Galileo's critics had misunderstood scripture and had mistakenly taken it as not only fact, but religious doctrine, that the earth must be the center of the universe. As a result, John Paul II declared the church had made a mistake in condemning Galileo.

36. I know that there were revolutions to overthrow kings in America, France, and England. Did these attacks hurt the papacy, too?

Yes. The very idea of an absolute or divine-right monarch was under attack. Early modern Europe and America saw battles between the forces of constitutionalism, which moved faster in

Great Britain than anywhere else given its history of Parliament, and absolutism, which recovered its hold on central Europe into the nineteenth century and reappeared in its worst form, as totalitarianism, in the twentieth century with Hitler, Stalin, and Mussolini. Constitutionalism benefited from the Enlightenment idea of liberalism as it related to many fields, especially politics and government, economics, and intellectual inquiry. Liberalism in this context does not fit into the modern Western divide of conservative vs. liberal, but it is the idea that humans should be free (from the Latin, *liber*) to run their own affairs, from the personal sphere to the level of national self-government, without outside interference.

Building on Enlightenment thinkers like the British political philosophers Thomas Hobbes (1588–1679) and John Locke (1632–1704), who strongly influenced America's Founding Fathers, political and religious writers overturned the notion that one person or family should rule because God says so. Self-determination (not quite full democracy yet, because women, the lower classes, and slaves were excluded) was the political battle cry that led to revolutions in 1688 in Great Britain, in 1776 in America, and in 1789 in France. Because kings were successfully overthrown, some saw the pope as just another monarch, perhaps the worst example of divine-right monarchy if you opposed the idea. For some Enlightenment writers who challenged the idea of a God, or at least of a God involved in the details of everyday life, the religious underpinning of a Christian monarchy called the papacy collapsed, as well.

37. How did European countries try to take over the church?

Nothing new here: monarchs had been trying to control the church in their territories since Constantine. What happened in these early modern centuries recalls the medieval actions of Charlemagne, the Ottos and Henrys, William the Conqueror, Philip the Fair, and Henry VIII among many others. At this time, the clergy and national governments were taking actions to step away from Roman authority and to set up self-determining state commissions or departments for church affairs in their lands. In France, with its long history of struggle between pope and king, a series of *Gallican Articles* (or *Liberties*) codified what had been brewing as Gallicanism for centuries. In 1682, the French clergy asserted that France was indeed a Catholic country in terms of doctrine, but not discipline: the French government and bishops, not the pope in Rome, controlled how the church would be run within the country. This meant that the king, not the pope, was head of the French church, which was in essence just another state department or bureaucracy. Gallicanism also reached back to the Council of Constance and the most virulent strain of conciliarism, declaring that only a council and not the pope was infallible. The French clergy explicitly rejected the idea that the pope had legitimate temporal authority by stating: "St. Peter and the popes, his successors, and the church itself have received dominion from God only over things spiritual and such as concern salvation, and not over things temporal and civil. Hence kings and sovereigns are not by God's command subject to any ecclesiastical dominion in things temporal."[49] Continuing this history of Gallican independence, the French revolutionaries, in the *Civil Constitution of the Clergy* in 1790, redrew the boundaries of dioceses, abolished appeals to Rome's authority, and made bishops and priests elected civil servants who had to take a loyalty oath to the state and deny the pope's power over them. Later, more radical revolutionaries dissolved monasteries and convents, raped nuns, murdered priests and religious, stole church property, and outlawed the Christian calendar, feast days, and sacraments.

There were other similar attempts to control the Catholic church in Europe. In Austria, the emperor Joseph II (1765–90) declared he would name bishops in his territory, redraw the boundaries of parishes and dioceses, and, like William the Conqueror in England about 700 years earlier, veto papal letters to believers in his lands. Austrians separated religious orders in their territories from their Roman headquarters and dissolved about a third of the convents and monasteries.[50] German bishops declared that they were in charge of the German church in a movement called Febronianism after the pseudonym of an auxiliary bishop in Trier, who wrote in 1763 that the pope was the center of unity who could step in when bishops failed in their duties, but that a pope should normally act in a collegial and not a monarchical manner, that is, the way popes acted (according to this account) before becoming political and temporal after crowning Charlemagne emperor in 800. The pope was subject to a council, as well, although he was the one to carry out its decrees like a delegated minister. Febronius also wanted national synods and the ability to remove or restrict interfering papal nuncios.[51]

38. Did Napoleon really take the popes prisoners?

Yes, Napoleon took two successive popes as prisoners in a kind of house arrest: Pius VI (1775–99) and Pius VII (1800–1823). The context, as we've seen for the last few questions and answers, indicates a weak papacy that had trouble gaining the loyalty of its own clergy, let alone monarchs and national governments eager to use religion as the glue for their own societies or to deemphasize religion altogether. Pius VI was more interested in demanding obedience than in winning respect; he was also more successful in supporting the arts than his clergy. Napoleon did not try to discard Christianity; he called Pius VII to crown him emperor in Paris, after all, though he snatched the crown off the altar and put it on himself. But he did want to be in charge of the church in France and wherever else his ambitions led. When Napoleon invaded Italy, his men took into custody Pius VI, who died in exile in French territory.

Things were so bad that some in Europe thought they'd seen the end of the papacy. Nevertheless, a conclave met under Austrian oversight in Venice, the last time a conclave was held outside Rome. After almost seven months, the longest time without a pope in recent memory, Pius VII was elected. The new pope did not think democratic and Christian ideas were incompatible; he had also voiced support for aspects of toleration and liberalism. When surrounded by a strong team of advisers, Pius VII was smarter, shrewder, and tougher than his predecessor; he returned the papacy to Rome within a few months of his election. Once Napoleon grew tired of Pius VII's attempts at political neutrality and independence, and angered by the pope's excommunication of those he called Peter's robbers, the emperor repeated his prior steps against the papacy: he invaded Italy, seized Pius VII as a prisoner in 1809, and isolated him from the advisers who made him decisive. After a few years, under pressure the pope signed a document apparently giving up the papal states, but shortly thereafter took back this decision. Meanwhile, Napoleon's fortunes had peaked and fallen: as a result, Pius VII was released and returned to Rome in 1814.

39. How did Catholics respond?

People rally round their leaders when their country or faith is attacked: unpopular politicians know that nothing will send their polls rising as quickly as a military action against an enemy posing imminent danger. Even those Catholics who recognized the papacy's weaknesses and the failures of individual popes saw the treatment of Pius VI and Pius VII as shameful. Ironically, the capture of a weak man such as Pius VI boosted support for the papacy, however tired and worldly it had become. As the papal historian Eamon Duffy summed it up: "Martyrdom wipes all scores clean, and in the eyes of the world Pius VI died a martyr."[52] Elected at the potential brink of the papacy's very existence, Pius VII knew that, however much he had to act politically to safeguard the church, the papacy's renewal would come through religion and not power. Those who had counted the papacy out had not reckoned with the very supportive reaction of some Catholics, which came to be called ultramontanism, against their popes' mistreatment.[53]

40. What's ultramontanism?

Ultramontanists reacted against nationalism, a movement that had been brewing for centuries and exploded during the early modern period. Nationalism placed a person's country, nationality, ethnic identity, or culture as his or her ultimate loyalty. Many Catholics, in response, embraced a position that came to be called ultramontanism, which went beyond nationalism. The word *ultramontanism* literally translated means "beyond/over the mountains," referring in this case to the Alps that separate the Italian peninsula from the rest of continental Europe. The word has come to indicate a very strong loyalty to the person of the pope, a hypernationalism wherein a person's identity as a Catholic fully obedient to the pope trumps any other claim to loyalty and identity: language, culture, society, ethnicity, race, geography, national borders, political affiliation, or government. The primary allegiance is to the sitting pope and to the papacy as an institution. Ultramontanism flowed both ways. A Catholic's loyalty flowed over that person's national borders to the pope in Rome. The pope's appeal transcended borders, too: it flowed outward from Rome, up and over the Alps, and throughout the world.

Ultramontanism was very much a reaction to both nationalism and to the rough treatment the papacy had received in the late eighteenth and early nineteenth centuries. While the papacy's poor reputation was at times justified, some people chose to respond by proverbially accentuating the positive and eliminating the negative, which was precisely the strategy Robert Bellarmine had adopted with some success after the Protestant reformations. In its extreme form, ultramontanism led the most ardent papal defenders and followers to the topic of papal infallibility (which we will take up in part II of this book). For now, we should note that ultramontanism makes a direct connection between the papacy and Catholic loyalty: you cannot be fully loyal to one without being completely loyal to the other. This connection poses a problem, of course, for readers aware of papal errors, missteps, and even schism or heresy. The reaction or even overreaction—and this is what ultramontanism can turn out to be—is an allegiance to the pope that makes the man seem more than human, but just below God: God's mouthpiece or an unassailable prophet. Ultramontanism, indeed, could lead to something like an unseemly veneration, even worship, of the man sitting as Peter's successor, a cult of Peter or the pope that comes dangerously close to crossing a line reserved only for God in Catholic theology.

41. It seems that some popes were afraid of modernity and others weren't. Is this true?

Yes, that's true, but we must remember that the pace of change in the nineteenth and twentieth centuries was stunning. Few people, let alone institutions, could keep up. Movements for greater political participation were exciting and represented progress, to be sure, but they also produced social upheaval and violence, which is why revolutions seeking radical change are often followed by counterrevolutions or reactionaries supporting a return to the previous status quo. In such circumstances, sticking with what has lasted can be a wise choice. Only over time can new ideas be proven worthy or trendy.

The poster-child pope for holding the line against Enlightenment liberalism is Gregory XVI (1831–46). He was a reactionary and an absolutist's absolutist, perhaps elected for just that reason. Earlier in his career, he had vigorously defended Pius VI, the right of the papacy to hold temporal authority, and the church's freedom against "the attacks of innovators." As pope, he prohibited the use of the new railroads in the papal states, calling them tracks to hell, and opposed participatory government, nationalism, liberalism, free speech, and the separation of church and state that was becoming the norm. When the rallying cry throughout the world, and even within parts of the church, was a progressive call for reform and renewal, Gregory dismissed the very idea that the church needed reform because such a statement would be based on the premise that she had become deformed. This, the pope said, was simply not possible.[54]

At the same time, however, he was not at all opposed to evangelization—not surprising from a man who had once headed the Vatican's department for spreading the faith. Under his leadership, the church's missionary activity exploded: he favored missionary orders, created about seventy dioceses and other church territories around the world, appointed almost two hundred bishops in mission territories, and supported efforts to turn leadership over to indigenous priests and bishops as quickly as possible.

As far as this issue of modernism goes, it's hard to define the term. Boiled down to a simple, if even simplistic, definition, modernism was an open approach to new developments in politics (constitutionalism), liberalism (freedom of speech, press, assembly), and intellectual inquiry. It was this last topic that led some Catholic modernists into trouble. They were using more scientific academic methods to study scripture, the history of Jews and Christians, archaeology, and theology in an attempt to capture what really happened during biblical times and then throughout church history. These critical methods did not criticize the church, but required that not everything should be taken on faith alone. Traditions and legends needed to have their roots unearthed. Modernists wanted to know the historical contexts of Jesus, theological developments, and the church's heroes and villains. They believed the human aspects of the church could and should change, but they also acknowledged eternal truths.[55]

Many modernists were reformers, and popes like Gregory XVI were often skittish about their methods and suspicious of them personally. In 1864, Pius IX (1846–78) listed a series of modernist propositions, which were summarized in a clumsy and imprecise way, and condemned this "Syllabus of Errors," including rationalism, liberalism, capitalism, freedom of inquiry and expression, and socialism. Leo XIII may have opened the Vatican's archives, but he declared in 1893 that it was impossible for there to be errors in the Bible. Under Pius X (1903–14), all Catholics had to believe Moses wrote the first five books of the Bible, known as the Pentateuch, even though the last few verses of the fifth book, Deuteronomy, describe his death and burial. Like Pius IX before him, Pius X gathered a list of errors—often blanket statements taken out of context—for condemnation. These actions allowed secret investigations and self-appointed (often anti-intellectual) watchdogs into seminaries, parishes, and lecture halls, which led to professors and priests being blacklisted and denounced in Rome without knowing their accusers or reviewing the evidence against them. This shameful witch-hunt accused nearly anyone regardless of rank or scholarly reputation, leading to whisper campaigns, self-censorship, and a chilling effect on Catholic intellectual life that sent many of the brightest lights underground. Pius X, however, saw himself as a champion not only of orthodoxy against what he called a synthesis of every other heresy, but as a pope whose job it was to demand and obtain absolute obedience, even intellectual submission. Modernism was a dragon and he was the St. George who would slay it.

The tide, however, would turn. The next two popes, the conciliatory Benedict XV (1914–22) and the scholarly Pius XI (1922–39), stopped the secret investigations, rehabilitated some of the Catholic thinkers harmed by the modernist witch-hunt, and encouraged responsible scholarship. Pius XII (1939–58) was especially interested in the revival of liturgy that was based in sound study on the early church; he also encouraged the use of modern methodologies to explore scripture and resist fundamentalist interpretations. John XXIII (1958–63) called Vatican II, which was not quite the triumph of modernism that some would say it was, although many of the ideas and approaches that had been denounced by antimodernist supporters were revived at the council. Ironically, when he was elected pope, John XXIII discovered that there was a file on him dating back to his early career as a church history professor at an Italian seminary. He recalled being denounced at that time for having students read a church history textbook that used modern approaches. And certainly no pope was more modern, at least in terms of using cutting-edge technology, than John Paul II, who recorded CDs, wrote bestsellers, put the Vatican online, and played the mass media like a maestro.

42. Was Pius XII really "Hitler's pope"?

This is a difficult question, and it's really not a fair one. The answer must be no. To use some parallels: Pius VI and Pius VII weren't Napoleon's popes, nor was Leo III Charlemagne's pope. Some of my colleagues think even addressing the matter this way is not the right starting point because, they say, to accept the question implicitly legitimates the accusation. "Hitler's pope" is, indeed, a loaded phrase, not unlike: "So when did you stop beating your wife?" But it is a question Catholics hear frequently, and so we must address it.

The phrase comes from the deliberately incendiary title of a 1999 book, *Hitler's Pope: The Secret History of Pius XII,* that sold well but was criticized by many scholars as a sloppy and unbalanced journalistic attempt at scholarship.[56] The notion that Pius XII was somehow in Hitler's pocket is allegedly based on the years Pius XII had spent as a diplomat in Germany before his election to the papacy and his admiration of German culture. The charges against Pius XII, however, surfaced well before this book, even to the time of World War II and the Shoah (the preferred word for Holocaust in the Jewish community) itself; critics argue that the pope did not do enough to save Jews and that he failed in his moral leadership. Others cite a history of anti-Semitism within Christianity that cannot be denied. What some call a systematic smear campaign against Pius XII dates to a play from the early 1960s, Rolf Hochhuth's *The Deputy,* which depicted Pius XII as criminally silent and complicit during the Shoah. The reaction to the play was resurrected by the 1999 book.

There is a variety of opinions, of course, with two extremes. Those who want to blame the Shoah on the church see a fall guy in Pius XII. Those who always defend the church, no matter what, see an anti-Catholic conspiracy in the accusation. Between are many opinions and questions. The Catholic church's quiet and heroic record in doing much to aid Jews during the Shoah has been well documented, recognized, and praised by many mainstream secular and religious Jews. But over the centuries, Christianity contributed to a culture of anti-Semitism, as John Paul II himself noted. Could the church and Pius XII have done more? Has the Vatican been as forthcoming as it might be in allowing access to the relevant documents? Are records even available, given the dangerous times?

As with any controversy, no response will satisfy everyone. History needs time and distance from this issue, and we simply have not had enough yet. Only preliminary assessments can be offered. The best thing to do is to read more about the debate and to decide for yourself, being careful to draw from responsible scholarship and opinion while avoiding polemics or material that prejudges the matter from any angle.[57]

43. Recent popes seem to have been very different types of men, no?

Yes, but that's not surprising. We have seen runs of the same type of men in church history, as in the medieval monarchs and the early modern administrators, but even within those groups there were many different personalities: bombastic and quiet men; scholars and humanists; leaders of simple spirituality, mystics, pastors; the greedy and the generous; popes with big egos and true humility. Other eras saw contrasting popes in close proximity, particularly a set of Pauls from the time of the Reformation. Paul III (1534–49) and Paul IV (1555–59) were both Italian aristocrats, patrons, and clients of the Renaissance papacy in all its excess. But though they shared a papal name and reigned within a short time of each other, a more contrasting approach to the Protestants could not be found. Paul III was well aware that some criticisms and calls for reform leveled by both Protestants and Catholics were well justified; in response, he created a climate for reform in Rome, calling in outsiders to tell the curia and papal machinery just what was wrong with them. Paul IV, on the other hand, was the father of the Counter-Reformation: a hard-headed approach that took the Protestants as wrong, the Catholics as right, and a zero-sum end game as the battleground. He backed the Inquisition and the Index of Forbidden Books while acting in an oppressive, defensive, and monarchical manner.

We find the same model of contrast in the last 150 years or so. Pius IX (1846–78) was a social and political conservative while Leo XIII (1878–1903) shared Pius' monarchical tendencies but also promoted social Catholicism and generally supported intellectual inquiry (with some important exceptions; see question 41). Pius X (1903–14) slew the modernist dragon like his namesake Pius IX, but Benedict XV (1914–22) took off some of the chill. He was diplomatic, certainly a necessary attribute given World War I, which began the month before his election. His successor Pius XI (1922–39) permitted scholarship to continue, but was only partially successful at defending the church against the rise of Italian fascism. However, he showed a human face to a world hit by the Depression and promoted clerical-lay partnership and social Catholicism, like Leo XIII before him, even while being every bit the monarch that his predecessors had been. Pius XII (1939–58) was an austere man, again a diplomat elected during the tensions that produced a world war, and he was followed by the grandfatherly John XXIII (1958–63). In turn, Paul VI (1963–78) was another introvert and diplomat who saw himself as indecisive and wondered if he was a Don Quixote tilting at windmills—a man who didn't disagree with John XXIII's earlier assessment of him as a Hamlet. While John Paul I (1978) was pope for just a month, it did appear that his personality was warmer than Paul VI's and he was quickly dubbed the smiling pope. John Paul II's big, brash, extroverted papacy was followed by Benedict XVI's quieter, introverted style.

44. Everybody said Pope John Paul II traveled more than any other pope in history. Is this true and what is the importance of all those trips?

Despite all the comments that Pope John Paul II was the most widely traveled pope in history, which is true, it was not at all unusual for medieval popes to live away from Rome for long stretches of time. In a pre-media age, popes had to move around in order to involve themselves directly in church affairs, lead local councils, and make their presence known. Pre-modern kings, queens, emperors, and empresses did this all the time, too, on what were called royal progresses.

The importance of travel for modern popes cannot be underestimated. The events during these trips should not be dismissed as merely symbolic. The popes are no longer prisoners of the Vatican or alleged puppets of France or Italy. In 1964, Paul VI became the first pope since Peter to walk in the Holy Land. He traveled to Constantinople in 1967 to celebrate, with Ecumenical Patriarch Athenagoras I, the 1965 lifting of the mutual excommunications of East and West dating back to 1054. Paul VI took the papacy to the United Nations, the poverty of India, and the swiftly growing Catholic populations of the Far East. The Polish John Paul II, a man who lived for many years under Nazi occupation and Soviet authority, prayed at Auschwitz, visited the Shoah memorial in Israel, and celebrated a huge outdoor Mass in Communist Cuba.

The church has grown to become truly global. If she is to flourish, communication and physical contact must be symbiotic, moving from the church's center of Rome to her periphery around the world and then back again. The pope visiting ancient cities and newly developing countries demonstrates that the church is both old and new at the same time. Ironically, because of the immediacy and speed offered by modern technology and the mass media—especially the Internet—the pope doesn't have to leave the Vatican to be seen and heard around the world. But Paul VI and John Paul II, especially, believed that the papacy should come to the people, not the other way around. John Paul II even explained his frequent traveling by saying people have a right to see their pope.

PART II

Power and Symbols, Cardinals and Conclaves

A. Papal Authority

45. I heard that Pope John Paul II called for a discussion about papal primacy. What *is* papal primacy?

Before we get to the discussion, we must first define some important vocabulary, in particular that word *primacy* and a partner word in the conversation, *supremacy*. Primacy means someone or something comes or goes first, ahead of other things, in terms of priority or honor. Supremacy means that someone has authority above everyone else. The two words do not always mean the same thing. A firstborn child, for instance, might have primacy plus supremacy; indeed, in many cultures (at least in the past) the eldest son or daughter had certain responsibilities and privileges. An eldest son might be his father's heir, even to a throne, while an eldest daughter might not marry, or will wait until later in life, because it is considered her responsibility to care for aging parents. But this is not always true. Sometimes a younger sibling, who does not have primacy because of birth order, takes on a sort of supremacy in caretaking or in being the family mediator or leader because of personality, demeanor, or unforeseen circumstances.

In terms of our topic, the scriptural passages we discussed in the first two questions of this book seem to indicate that Peter had primacy because Jesus singled him out and placed him above the other apostles as head of the church. For Catholic theology, primacy is also composed of supremacy: Peter and his successors, the popes, are first in honor, rank, and authority. The papal authority is supreme, although both the pope and all the bishops are equally bishops. A pope is not "more bishop" than a bishop of a diocese or an auxiliary (assistant) bishop, but the pope's mandate—his job and responsibility—is broader. He is the bishop of the diocese of Rome, yes, but he is also the universal shepherd, which is a role that only he and no other bishop bears. This role stems precisely from his position as bishop of Rome, where Peter is buried.

In his 1995 encyclical, *Ut unum sint,* Pope John Paul II asked for continuing study and dialogue about the papacy:

> Could not the real but imperfect communion existing between [Christian communities] persuade church leaders and their theologians to engage with me in a patient and fraternal dialogue on this subject, a dialogue in which, leaving useless controversies behind, we could listen to one another, keeping before us only the will of Christ for his Church and allowing ourselves to be deeply moved by his plea "that they may all be one...so that the world may believe that you have sent me" (John 17:21)?[1]

This invitation led some to wonder if this was a serious or disingenuous suggestion because the historical and theological equation of papal primacy with papal supremacy has led to questions and even conflicts.[2] The papacy, primacy, and supremacy are serious challenges for Catholics and her ecumenical partners. Orthodox and Protestants place these topics among the central reasons why full Christian unity cannot exist; most Roman Catholic Christians will not give up the belief that papal primacy equals papal supremacy. However, the encyclical itself shows a willingness for the Catholic church to reform the papacy to serve Christian unity, even before all of the theological issues have been resolved.

The status of the papacy will probably remain a serious sticking point in ecumenical attempts to bring Christians together, although there have been remarkable results in dialogues between Roman Catholics and Anglicans, Lutherans, Methodists, and the Orthodox in America. A series of Lutheran-Roman Catholic dialogues in the late 1960s and early 1970s produced statements like the following that are surprising for showing just how much

Lutherans and Catholics agree on when it comes to the papacy, although no one is denying fundamental disagreements:

> While we have concluded that traditional sharp distinctions between divine and human institutions are no longer useful, Catholics continue to emphasize that papal primacy is an institution in accordance with God's will. For Lutherans this is a secondary question. The one thing necessary, they insist, is that papal primacy serve the gospel and that its exercise of power not subvert Christian freedom.[3]

Meanwhile, some within Roman Catholicism took up the pope's call for critique and offered ideas for reforming the curia and papacy.[4]

46. Pope Benedict XVI dropped the title "patriarch of the west." What's the significance of this?

Let's review some historical background that's related to the prior question of primacy and supremacy. The pope has many titles: bishop of Rome, vicar of Jesus Christ, successor of the prince of the apostles, supreme pontiff of the universal church, primate of Italy, archbishop and metropolitan archbishop of the Roman province, sovereign of the State of Vatican City, and servant of the servants of God.[5] Up until Benedict XVI, the pope also held the title patriarch of the west. This last title appears as patriarch of Rome as well as patriarch of the west in documents throughout history. The first version, patriarch of Rome, recalls the fact that the early church recognized a certain leadership among the bishops of the five most important and prestigious cities of the ancient Mediterranean world: Rome, Antioch, Alexandria, Constantinople, and Jerusalem. A few centuries after Jesus' lifetime, when the Roman Empire was split in half in order to administer it more efficiently, Rome in the west and Constantinople in the east emerged as the most important two of the five patriarchates, hence the pope's title moving to patriarch of the west, a phrase eventually for-malized by Pope Theodore I (642–49).

In February 2006, about a year after his election as pope, Benedict XVI decided to drop this title patriarch of the west. His action caused some confusion, even consternation, as it was initially taken as an attempt at raw power—that is, to raise himself above ancient categories and stress his primacy and supremacy. Within a few weeks, however, explanations for the move came out of the Vatican emphasizing the pope's hope that removing the title would promote, not block, ecumenical dialogue and collegiality. In fact, the explanation came through the office of the Pontifical Council for Promoting Christian Unity. In summary, the office said Benedict thinks the title no longer applies, because the world is no longer split into east and west in the ancient geographic manner. Moreover, the explanation said the phrase patriarch of the west doesn't describe quite accurately his jurisdiction (primacy and supremacy) over the Roman Catholic (or Latin) church and the Eastern churches that are in communion with her. The pope's authority is not the same over all the churches in communion with Rome. Eastern churches enjoy an autonomy not shared by those in the west. How best to describe both of these relationships remains an open question.

47. If the pope is the highest authority in the church, what is the authority of my local bishop or a group of bishops?

This question leads us to the issue of episcopal (from the Greek *episcopos* and Latin *episcopus* for bishop) collegiality: the authority and power that each bishop shares as a member of the college of bishops in communion and unity with the pope.[6] Vatican II in 1964 issued a document titled *Lumen gentium,* which treats the topic of papal authority within the context of the college of bishops. Because of their importance and the organic, integrated nature of the theology underlying them, we must quote the critical passages at length.

Episcopal consecration, together with the office of sanctifying, also confers the office of teaching and of governing, which, however, of its very nature, can be exercised only in hierarchical communion with the head [the pope] and the members of the college [of bishops]....Just as in the Gospel, the Lord so disposing, St. Peter and the other apostles constitute one apostolic college, so in a similar way the Roman pontiff, the successor of Peter, and the bishops, the successors of the apostles, are joined together....But the college or body of bishops has no authority unless it is understood together with the Roman pontiff, the successor of Peter as its head. The pope's power of primacy over all, both pastors and faithful, remains whole and intact. In virtue of his office, that is as vicar of Christ and pastor of the whole Church, the Roman pontiff has full, supreme and universal power over the Church. And he is always free to exercise this power. The order of bishops, which succeeds to the college of apostles and gives this apostolic body continued existence, is also the subject of supreme and full power over the universal Church, provided we understand this body together with its head the Roman pontiff and never without this head. This power can be exercised only with the consent of the Roman pontiff. For our Lord placed Simon alone as the rock and the bearer of the keys of the Church, and made him shepherd of the whole flock; it is evident, however, that the power of binding and loosing, which was given to Peter, was granted also to the college of apostles, joined with their head. This college, insofar as it is composed of many [bishops], expresses the variety and universality of the people of God, but insofar as it is assembled under one head [the pope], it expresses the unity of the flock of Christ. In it, the bishops, faithfully recognizing the primacy and pre-eminence of their

head, exercise their own authority for the good of their
own faithful, and indeed of the whole church, the Holy
Spirit supporting its organic structure and harmony
with moderation....The Roman pontiff, as the successor of Peter, is the perpetual and visible principle and
foundation of unity of both the bishops and of the
faithful. The individual bishops, however, are the visible
principle and foundation of unity in their particular
churches, fashioned after the model of the universal
Church, in and from which churches come into being
the one and only Catholic Church. For this reason the
individual bishops represent each his own church, but
all of them together and with the pope represent the
entire Church in the bond of peace, love and unity.
The individual bishops, who are placed in charge of
particular churches, exercise their pastoral government
over the portion of the people of God committed to
their care, and not over other churches nor over the
universal church. But each of them, as a member of
the episcopal college and legitimate successor of the
apostles, is obliged by Christ's institution and command to be solicitous for the whole church, and this
solicitude, though it is not exercised by an act of jurisdiction, contributes greatly to the advantage of the universal church. For it is the duty of all bishops to
promote and to safeguard the unity of faith and the discipline common to the whole church, to instruct the
faithful to love for the whole mystical body of Christ,
especially for its poor and sorrowing members and for
those who are suffering persecution for justice's sake,
and finally to promote every activity that is of interest
to the whole church, especially that the faith may take
increase and the light of full truth appear to all men.

Perhaps because of concerns that the pope's authority had seemingly been watered down by these passages concerning episcopal collegiality, an explanatory note issued "by higher authority" (almost certainly Pope Paul VI and surely with his approval) and without input from Vatican II's bishops was added at the last minute to *Lumen gentium*. This note emphasized the bishops' dependence on the pope for their assignments and for the exercise of their authority as well as the pope's independence from the college, his direction of the college, and his higher place in the hierarchy. Bishops can act together collegially only at certain times; the pope can act fully and independently at will.[7]

So a delicate balancing act must take place: while the pope is a member of the college of bishops as a bishop, he is at the same time the head of that college as pope. The college of bishops cannot operate without its head. As the *Code of Canon Law* (1983), following the language of *Lumen gentium* closely, puts it: "The college of bishops, whose head is the Supreme Pontiff...together with its head and never without this head, is also the subject of supreme and full power over the universal church."[8] The pope, however, is not similarly bound, although many bishops assume that when the pope defines a dogma, he will do so in communion with his brother bishops.

> The bishop of the Roman church, in whom continues the office given by the Lord uniquely to Peter, the first of the apostles, and to be transmitted to his successors, is the head of the college of bishops, the vicar of Christ, and the pastor of the universal Church on earth. By virtue of his office he possesses supreme, full, immediate, and universal ordinary power in the Church, which he is always able to exercise freely....By virtue of his office, the Roman pontiff not only possesses power over the universal church but also obtains the primacy of ordinary power over all particular churches and groups of them. Moreover, this primacy strengthens and pro-

tects the proper, ordinary, and immediate power which
bishops possess in the particular churches entrusted to
their care. In fulfilling the office of supreme pastor of the
church, the Roman pontiff is always joined in communion with the other bishops and with the universal
Church. He nevertheless has the right, according to the
needs of the Church, to determine the manner, whether
personal or collegial, of exercising this office.[9]

In *Ut unum sint,* issued a little more than a decade after the
Code of Canon Law and three decades after *Lumen gentium,* John
Paul II continued to strike the balance between episcopal collegiality, on the one hand, and papal primacy and supremacy, on the
other. John Paul II noted specifically that he and his brother bishops share the task of unity, but that the pope takes a leadership
position for the sake of that unity.

> With the power and the authority without which such
> an office would be illusory, the bishop of Rome must
> ensure the communion of all the churches. For this rea-
> son, he is the first servant of unity....It is the responsi-
> bility of the successor of Peter to recall the requirements
> of the common good of the church, should anyone be
> tempted to overlook it in the pursuit of personal inter-
> ests. He has the duty to admonish, to caution and to
> declare at times that this or that opinion being circu-
> lated is irreconcilable with the unity of faith. When cir-
> cumstances require it, he speaks in the name of all the
> pastors in communion with him....All this however
> must always be done in communion. When the
> Catholic church affirms that the office of the bishop of
> Rome corresponds to the will of Christ, she does not
> separate this office from the mission entrusted to the
> whole body of bishops, who are also "vicars and ambas-
> sadors of Christ" [Vatican II, *Lumen gentium,* 27]. The

bishop of Rome is a member of the "college," and the bishops are his brothers in the ministry.[10]

48. What are episcopal conferences, and what is their authority with respect to the pope's authority?

Bishops come together regularly in episcopal conferences in an individual country, such as the United States' bishops who meet twice each year, or in a region, like Latin America's CELAM conference (an acronym for Consejo Episcopal Latinoamericano). At these meetings, the bishops usually discuss particular challenges—such as the priest-pedophilia crimes and episcopal coverups that dominated the American bishops' meeting in Dallas in June 2002—or common topics like religious education or liturgy.[11]

Bishops also gather in synods typically held in Rome to address a specific topic. Synods were established in their modern form in 1965 by Paul VI, though records from the church's past use words like *synod* or *council,* usually informally or imprecisely, to identify the local and regional gatherings of bishops that have always been an essential feature of the church's life.[12] Today, synods are composed of representatives of the world's bishops or of those from a particular continent or region; unlike episcopal conferences, synods are not deliberative bodies where bishops vote. They serve as places where bishops and the pope can enter into dialogue with each other in what amounts to a massive consultation or information-gathering session. Also unlike the national or regional episcopal conferences, synods are papal events: they are called and run by the Vatican, not by the bishops of a particular area themselves. (Some dioceses also hold their own local synods, but these are intramural events.)

The status of national episcopal conferences came up for discussion in 1985, when John Paul II called representatives of the world's bishops together to reassess how the implementation of Vatican II's teachings was proceeding. There had been concern in the intervening two decades that national episcopal conferences might be places where, inadvertently or not, the idea of a national Catholicism might be cultivated, instead of a Roman Catholicism that is universal. Some wondered just how authoritative such bishops' conferences were. Cardinal Joseph Ratzinger (the future Pope Benedict XVI), while working as Prefect of the Congregation for the Doctrine of the Faith under John Paul II, wrote in 1986, "We must not forget that the episcopal conferences have no theological basis; they do not belong to the structure of the church as willed by Christ, that cannot be eliminated; they have only a practical, concrete function."[13]

It took many years for the Vatican to consider and respond to these developments and issues; not until 1998 did John Paul II publish an apostolic letter, *Apostolos suos*, about episcopal conferences. He stated that national or regional episcopal conferences have a limited authority in terms of doctrine and exercise a partial collegiality, not the full collegiality exercised when all of the world's bishops gather with the pope. John Paul II allowed episcopal conferences to establish binding policies and decisions only if they had been passed by a unanimous vote of the whole body of bishops in that conference. If a statement received a two-thirds majority, the statement could stand provided that it was subsequently approved by the Vatican.[14]

49. What about general councils like Vatican II?

There have been twenty-one general councils in the church's life.[15] Before many of them met, smaller councils of bishops gathered locally to identify, discuss, and try to meet doctrinal and disciplinary challenges. In this way, both problems and solutions bubbled from the church's body up to the higher levels of the hierarchy for decisions. We find this process, for example, in local synods of bishops held in the years before the general councils of Nicaea I (325) and Ephesus (431) produced official teachings, especially about the person of Jesus and the nature of Mary's motherhood. Other times, popes called a general council and requested that bishops meet in their locales beforehand to compare notes and send topics to Rome for the general council's agenda, which is what happened when Pope Innocent III (1198–1216) gave the bishops about a two-and-a-half year lead time to prepare for Lateran IV in Rome in 1215.

A general council of bishops cannot meet on its own authority. Current canon law declares that only the pope can call a general council into being, preside over it, or appoint someone to do so for him. His leadership was not always so clear and direct. During the church's first thousand years, Roman and Byzantine emperors (and one empress) called and presided over eight general councils, sometimes with papal participation if only through a legate. In addition, it is now law that only the pope can suspend or end its deliberations. A general council is automatically suspended if the pope dies during its meeting, which is what happened at Vatican II. That council decided in December 1962 to take a hiatus for committee work before meeting in a second session in autumn 1963. Pope John XXIII, who had called Vatican II, died in June 1963. His successor, Paul VI (1963–78) immediately said he would keep Vatican II on schedule. Also, currently only the pope controls the agenda, but he can make changes based on the bishops' suggestions. Finally, a very careful statement balances the bishops' role in decision-making with the pope's unique role in announcing those decisions and validating them: "The decrees of an ecumenical council do not have obligatory force unless they have been approved by the Roman Pontiff together with the council fathers [the bishops], confirmed by him, and promulgated at his order."[16]

50. Were things always so clear-cut?

No. Some bishops, theologians, church historians, and canon lawyers want more collaborative models of decision-making that provide greater respect for local authority and even a measure of autonomy. They can find examples of limited independence on the part of a region's bishops meeting in councils in church history. Specifically, the north African church of the third through fifth centuries serves as a paradigm for those who would like to see a modern Catholic church that allows local bishops and groups of bishops much more independence and authority. North Africa witnessed a very vibrant Christianity that survived Roman persecutions and enjoyed relative independence in the first few centuries of Christianity because of its distance from Rome. It was in north Africa (though not exclusively) that we find strong statements about each Christian community being autonomous, though connected by the faith to other Christian communities. In the first few centuries of the church, when Christianity was scattered and persecuted, the bishop was seen as the unifying head of the local church—to use a common phrase of the time: "Where the bishop is, there the church is"—and the concern was more on local survival than on universal communion.[17]

One of the most vocal spokesmen for this position was a controversial bishop in Carthage (modern-day Tunisia) named Cyprian, who was martyred in 258. In his writings, he asserted that the episcopate is a unity and that each bishop holds a part of the whole of that unity. Cyprian and many of his brother bishops in the area had respect, even reverence, for the bishop of Rome, but they addressed him as brother and not father. They did not think they had to defer to him or to send him their decisions for approval, basing their position largely on the interpretation of Pentecost that said the Holy Spirit came down equally on all of the apostles, so their successors— the bishops—shared power and authority equally. Cyprian was willing to say that Peter was a unifying source of the episcopacy, but not that Peter's primacy equaled supremacy.

Matters were not difficult as long as bishops agreed with each other. Cyprian enjoyed a fraternal correspondence with Cornelius in Rome (251–53), for instance, but then Cyprian and Stephen I (254–57) disagreed on whether people baptized by heretics should be baptized again. Stephen held that the original baptism was valid if it had been performed with water and in the name of the Trinity. Cyprian was more of a hard-liner, arguing that the baptism had not taken place because heretics could not pass along a faith they did not hold. Stephen, who may have been the first bishop of Rome to explicitly interpret Matthew 16:18 in terms of papal primacy, called Cyprian "false Christ" and "deceitful worker." Peter, Cyprian claimed in response, had not expressed his supremacy over Paul nor required his obedience. According to Cyprian, the church was founded on all the bishops and therefore pronounced himself shocked that one of them, the bishop of Rome, would claim to speak in the entire church's name. Interestingly, Cyprian originally had written his main document on church unity, *De catholicae ecclesiae unitate,* when he was in agreement with Cornelius. Several years later, during his conflict with Stephen, Cyprian rewrote key passages to deemphasize Peter's primacy and to say that whatever primacy existed did not connote supremacy, as well. In 256, Cyprian led a council against Stephen, declaring with a measure of defiance: "For no one of us sets himself up as a bishop of bishops nor by autocratic intimidation compels his colleagues to a forced obedience."[18]

A certain tradition of independence remained in north Africa for a few centuries, popping up periodically. In the early fifth century, for example, a priest of the region was deprived of his office by his bishop; the priest appealed to Zosimus (417–18) in Rome for reinstatement, but the north African bishops said the pope had no right to intervene. A few years later, in 424, the north African bishops gathered at a synod, revisited the incident, and issued a statement asserting their independence of Rome's Celestine I (422–32): "…[W]e earnestly entreat you for the future not to be ready to admit to a hearing persons that come from this region, nor to be willing to receive into communion those that have been excommunicated by us.…[A]ll causes should be concluded in the places where they arose."[19]

It was long the tradition, at least in north Africa, that Rome could confirm the decisions of local synods and thereby spread their impact. But local bishops were not usually comfortable when the pope asserted that decisions were not decisions until he said so—let alone when that pope in fact reversed the decisions made on the local level. In modern terms, such a position represents the principle of subsidiarity, which says that a matter should be resolved at the lowest, most local level without uninvited intervention from a higher level.[20]

51. But didn't St. Augustine say something like, "Rome has spoken, so the matter is closed"?

This is not the precise phrase and the difference matters, because this quotation is often used as a proof-text. However, it is taken out of context and misunderstood as a complete statement of absolute papal authority. The passage is from a sermon Augustine preached in 417 during an extremely confusing time when he and other north African bishops were fighting a heresy called Pelagianism, named after the theologian Pelagius, who spent his career in Rome and the Holy Land. The theological issues were complex and the historical record is unclear. Boiled down, it appears Pelagius believed Adam's sin was not passed down to all Christians, which meant that believers did not need baptism to wash away original sin; therefore, Jesus' death and resurrection were not required for redemption. If believers wanted to get to heaven, they had to lead almost perfect lives on their own, putting God's grace in a subordinate, even nonexistent position.

When two local synods in the Holy Land declared Pelagius was not a heretic, Augustine saw to it that another pair of local synods, this time in north Africa, condemned him. Looking to spread their important clarification of proper theology as widely as possible, the north African bishops sent public and private letters to Innocent I (401–17) in Rome, who concurred with the north African bishops' decision against Pelagius and excommunicated him. Augustine happily announced the news in a sermon: "In this matter the decision of two councils have been sent to the apostolic see. Letters have come thence as well. The case is finished."[21]

The interpretation of this statement, however, was not settled. North Africa's bishops, including Augustine, had probably looked to the bishop of Rome in the hope that his agreement with their condemnation of Pelagius would make their decision against the heresy apply to all of Christianity. Why? The answer is that Rome could trace its line back to the apostles, in this case Peter and Paul, while north Africa could not. Innocent, for his part, was pleased to receive the request because he took it as a sign that the north Africans were recognizing his authority over other bishops. As we have seen several times now, the north Africans cherished their independence, while deferring to a certain primacy in Rome that did not equal supremacy. Innocent may have seen the letters as implicit acknowledgments of his primacy as well as of his supremacy. One wonders what Augustine would have said had the Roman answer come back negating the actions of the north African bishops, who had sent their decision to Rome anticipating ratification and agreement, not as a formal appeal to a higher court.

52. What's an encyclical?

An encyclical is a particular form of writing, usually referred to informally as an open (or circular) letter, that popes use to communicate with their fellow bishops or even the entire world. It is, in this sense, more often an external communication with people outside the Vatican, the hierarchy, or even the worldwide Catholic population. Encyclicals date back several centuries, at least to Benedict XIV (1740–58), but it was only with Pius IX (1846–78) that encyclicals became more frequent. Leo XIII (1878–1903) especially utilized encyclicals to talk about a range of issues touching on people's everyday lives: marriage and family, social justice and labor, and the authority of civil power. As the twentieth century proceeded and the third millennium turned, popes increasingly used encyclicals to speak to the world.

The other famous papal document is a *bull*: a decision on a weighty matter that should be considered binding. Pope Leo X's condemnation of Martin Luther's theological positions in 1520, for example, took the form of a papal bull. The odd word comes from the Latin *bulla*, which refers to the heavy seal placed on the document. From the early Middle Ages on, the bull was the preferred form of papal document for the most serious matters.

53. What is papal infallibility?

It may seem strange to say so, but the best way to discuss papal infallibility is first to talk about what it is not, because it is one of the most misunderstood terms related to Catholicism. Moreover, it is misunderstood as much by Catholics as by non-Catholics.

In fact, the term itself is wrong. The formal explanation of the principle, which comes from the general council Vatican I (1869–70), reads: "On the infallible teaching authority of the Roman pontiff."[22] It is not the pope himself—as a human being, as a Catholic believer, or as a bishop—who is infallible, but the authority by which he teaches. Even here, the infallibility is restricted to the occasions when he makes a formal statement *ex cathedra,* meaning from his seat or chair of St. Peter—an important symbol of his teaching authority—on a matter of faith or morals. Such a statement is so rare that it has been invoked just once since Vatican I: in 1950, Pope Pius XII infallibly declared Mary's Assumption into heaven. Pope Pius IX formally declared in 1854 the teaching of Mary's Immaculate Conception. Although this statement predated the 1870 decision at Vatican I concerning the infallibility of the pope's teaching authority, theologians generally agree that it (and perhaps some prior declarations in church history, as well) was the equivalent of an *ex cathedra* statement.[23]

Looking back to question 52 for a moment, we should note that although an encyclical also comes directly from the pope himself, it is not the same as an *ex cathedra* statement made on a matter of faith or morals. The relative weight of various types of statements can be a bit murky. For instance, John Paul II in 1994 used the form of an apostolic letter, a less weighty document than an encyclical, to reassert in *Ordinatio sacerdotalis* that the church does not have the authority to ordain women into the priesthood. But he stated "that this judgment is to be definitively held by all the Church's faithful." This caused a great deal of discussion as to whether the subject was now entirely closed, even among theologians who agreed that only men could be ordained priests. In November 1995, the Congregation for the Doctrine of the Faith, with the pope's approval, issued a reply to the comments and questions that had been raised. It essentially said that the papal encyclical required the full assent of Catholics because the teaching that John Paul II's letter reiterated was itself infallible.[24]

Catholic theology gives the pope the opportunity to express a Catholic teaching infallibly on his own authority and without the consent of his brother bishops. Once again, Vatican II helps explain the issue in *Lumen gentium*:

> And this infallibility with which the Divine Redeemer willed his church to be endowed in defining doctrine of faith and morals, extends as far as the deposit of revelation extends, which must be religiously guarded and faithfully expounded. And this is the infallibility which the Roman pontiff, the head of the college of bishops, enjoys in virtue of his office, when, as the supreme shepherd and teacher of all the faithful, who confirms his brethren in their faith, by a definitive act he proclaims a doctrine of faith or morals. And therefore his definitions, of themselves, and not from the consent of the church, are justly styled irreformable, since they are pronounced with the assistance of the Holy Spirit, promised to him in blessed Peter, and therefore they need no approval of others, nor do they allow an appeal to any other judgment. For then the Roman pontiff is not pronouncing judgment as a private person, but as the supreme teacher of the universal Church, in whom the charism of infallibility of the Church itself is individually present, he is expounding or defending a doctrine of Catholic faith.

At the same time, the bishops share teaching authority (or *magisterium*) with the pope, even to the point of sharing in infallibility as long as they teach in communion and unity with the pope and are not expressing a teaching that contradicts him. As *Lumen gentium* says:

> The infallibility promised to the church resides also in the body of bishops, when that body exercises the supreme magisterium with the successor of Peter. To these definitions the assent of the church can never be wanting, on account of the activity of that same Holy Spirit, by which the whole flock of Christ is preserved and progresses in unity of faith.[25]

54. Where did the concept of papal infallibility come from?

For those who do not care for the idea of the pope's teaching authority being infallible, the answer will be "nowhere." But there is a long tradition of the church that declares dogmas to be infallible because they have been held by everyone, everywhere, at all times. Not every article of faith has been formally pronounced in an *ex cathedra* statement by a pope. You won't find, for example, a piece of papal stationery using this formula to declare that the Trinity is made up of Father, Son, and Holy Spirit, but who would doubt that this belief is a true and binding article of faith? Such statements are part of that long-standing, authoritative body of authentic Catholic teaching (generally coming from church councils), which contains what are identified as the articles or deposit of Catholic faith and morals.

In the Middle Ages, we find a few moments when popes seemed to be trying to give extra weight to their decisions. You'll recall from part I the list of twenty-seven statements appearing among the correspondence of Pope Gregory VII (1073–85) called the *Dictatus papae*. Item 22 declares: "That the Roman church has never erred, nor will it ever err, as scripture attests."[26] We should note that, in the Middle Ages, the "Roman church" was sometimes taken to mean the pope and cardinals, but at other times indicated our post-Reformation and modern term Roman Catholic Church: the entire church in communion with the pope in Rome. Popes who were fighting with the new religious order called the Franciscans in the twelfth and thirteenth centuries may have argued that their decisions concerning the controversial issue of just what poverty meant were authoritative because popes could not be wrong.[27] At the same time, other theologians including Thomas Aquinas seemed to regard the pope as the highest authority when teaching in communion with his brother bishops and especially when heading up a general council. It appears, then, that for many centuries the idea was that the church as a body could not fail, though individual Christians obviously could, given the human condition. The pope's role as ultimate witness and arbiter of infallible beliefs seemed to depend on the church's infallibility as an institution protected by God.[28]

The story of the teaching, however, really relates to Vatican I, which met in a post-Enlightenment world where the very idea of a monarchy, let alone a divine-right monarchy such as the papacy was sometimes described, came to be challenged by more participatory forms of government. Revolutions in America and France in the late eighteenth centuries were followed by periodic social unrest throughout Europe in the nineteenth century to such an extent that historians call 1848 the year of revolutions. Within this context, Pope Pius IX (1846–78) wanted to assert that the papacy was not just another monarchy and that the pope still held absolute power within the church. One might wonder fairly why, then, he called a council at all; why not simply make the declaration on his own? It appears that Pius IX wanted to make it clear that any statement on ultimate papal authority was supported by the world's bishops, who were called the pope's "co-assessors and fellow-judges" in Vatican I's other major document, the one that did not discuss infallibility and has subsequently been almost entirely overlooked.[29]

There were several groups of opinions about infallibility at Vatican I, with subtleties among them. To sum them up, perhaps too roughly, there was a small group of ultramontanists (see question 40) who wanted the strongest statement possible assigned to the infallibility of the pope himself and not just his teaching office. The bishop of Geneva put the matter flatly when he said that Jesus had three incarnations: in his mother's womb, in the Eucharist, and in "the old man in the Vatican." A British ultramontanist declared that he'd like to see an *ex cathedra* statement from the pope show up every morning with the newspaper on his breakfast table.[30] While another small group opposed the move altogether, most bishops backed the idea in principle but saw no need to have *ex cathedra* statements with any regularity. A good portion of these moderates, perhaps 20 percent, was called by the clumsy name inopportunists. These bishops, and the theologians who backed them, thought there was no need for such a definition of papal authority, arguing that the church had existed for centuries without one; that the definition would be a further impediment to union with non-Catholic Christians as well as confuse and maybe even divide Roman Catholics; and that the papacy's rocky history might not be able to support a strong statement of infallibility. After several months of fairly open debate and a few straw votes that indicated a strong minority of opposition, a statement was passed that said the pope's teaching authority, not the pope himself, was infallible. Infallibility applied not to every statement the pope made, such as those dealing with the church's discipline and administration as the ultramontanists wanted, but only to those related to matters of faith and morals. The pope's *ex cathedra* statements did not need approval by the church, which in practical terms meant a general council or the college of bishops: they were irreformable in and of themselves (a word repeated in *Lumen gentium* at Vatican II, as we just saw in question 53.)[31]

55. Did everyone agree with Vatican I?

There was, as we have noted, a significant minority of bishops who resisted the idea of infallibility as it was being discussed at the council. One Dominican theologian and cardinal delivered a nuanced opinion that, in fact, ended up carrying the day: the pope could issue an *ex cathedra* statement that enjoyed the charism of infallibility, but the pope himself was not an infallible human being. This cardinal asserted the pope's fellowship with the other bishops: although the pope was head of the college of bishops, he ought not to teach apart from them. Pressing his point, he said that bishops and the pope together shared a leading role in witnessing to the church's tradition. Late that night, this cardinal was summoned for a meeting with the pope. "I am tradition," Pius IX told him. "I am the church."[32] About sixty bishops were still uncomfortable enough that they decided to leave Rome rather than vote against the statement at a general council held in St. Peter's Basilica with the pope sitting right there. In the months and years after Vatican I, most of these bishops made public statements acknowledging the infallibility of the pope's teaching authority (it is assumed under pressure from Rome) and some saw their careers progress to the point of being made cardinals.

56. Popes *have* made mistakes. Wasn't one even condemned as a heretic?

It's natural to link papal mistakes with the issue of infallibility. We've already given a context that theoretically separates the pope as a man from the pope as the successor to St. Peter making an *ex cathedra* statement on a matter of faith and morals. In the common opinion of many, however, this is a distinction without a difference: most people do not separate the pope from every statement he utters despite the careful theology behind Vatican I and Vatican II teachings.

Yes, a pope was indeed condemned as a heretic. He was Pope Honorius I (625–38), who apparently believed that Jesus had only one will. After his death, this theological position was condemned as the heresy of monothelitism at a general council known as Constantinople III (680–81), which taught that Jesus had two wills, one divine and one human, to match his human and divine natures that are uniquely united into his one person. In sharp language, the council declared that Satan had been at work since the clarity achieved by the creeds of Nicaea I (325) and Constantinople I (381):

> But since, from the first, the contriver of evil did not rest, finding an accomplice in the serpent and through him bringing upon human nature the poisoned dart of death, so too now he has found instruments suited to his own purpose—namely [several bishops are named here] and further Honorius, who was pope of elder Rome, [other bishops named here]—and has not been idle in raising through them obstacles of error against the full body of the church,…

Another general council, Constantinople IV (869–70) reiterated that Jesus has two separate wills and then repeated the condemnation of Honorius by name.[33]

As you can imagine, there have been attempts to discount or explain Honorious. One position is that Honorius held this opinion as a private believer but that he never taught it publicly as pope: he did not seek to extend this belief to the body of the faithful or to make it an official church teaching. Some thought Honorius a benign though misguided leader. Others contended that while he did not hold this position at all, he did not fight hard enough to conquer it. The condemnation was not without its opponents at that time and at subsequent moments when the question of infallibility came up. Meanwhile, Honorius remains on the roll of true popes.

57. Pope John Paul II apologized for a lot of the church's mistakes, didn't he?

As part of the Jubilee Year 2000 celebrations, John Paul II publicly asked God for forgiveness—and forgave those who had harmed the church—during the Day of Pardon mass on March 12, 2000, which was the first Sunday of Lent. Interspersed with the pope's prayers, seven high-ranking cardinals and archbishops acknowledged the church's sins in general; those committed in the service of the truth, which most took to refer to inquisitions; sins that harmed the unity of Christ's body, appearing to mean the intra-Christian split since the Reformations; sins against the Jews; sins against "love, peace, the rights of peoples, and respect for cultures and religions"; sins against "the dignity of women and the unity of the human race"; and sins that trampled on human rights.[34]

This event drew worldwide attention, praise, and admiration except among the most cynical commentators within and outside Catholicism. But it was not the first time John Paul II had asked for forgiveness for the church: this Day of Pardon mass was simply the culmination of an effort he had undertaken from very early in his papacy. Historians should not make predictions, but I suspect that Pope John Paul II's acknowledgments of the church's mistakes will be a major part of his legacy and become more important as time passes. During his long papacy, he acknowledged the church's errors and asked God for forgiveness about one hundred times.[35] Gearing up for the Jubilee Year 2000 celebrations as early as 1994, he announced in an apostolic letter titled *Tertio millennio adveniente* that one of the best ways to prepare would be for believers as individuals and the church as an institution to undertake a collective examination of conscience:

> Hence it is appropriate that, as the second millennium of Christianity draws to a close, the church should become more fully conscious of the sinfulness of her children, recalling all those times in history when they departed from the spirit of Christ and his gospel and, instead of offering to the world the witness of a life inspired by the values of faith, indulged in ways of thinking and acting which were truly forms of counter-witness and scandal.[36]

As the Jubilee Year approached, John Paul II directed the International Theological Commission to prepare an explanation of the motives and theology behind his effort. In December 1999, the commission published a document titled "Memory and Reconciliation: The Church and the Faults of the Past."[37]

These documents and the form of these apologies are not without their flaws and critics, but one would be hard-pressed to find another institution taking such a public stand to acknowledge its historical mistakes.[38] There is, for instance, a consistent attempt to separate the actions of individuals, including church leaders, from the culpability of the church as an institution. This attempt can ring false when viewed through the prism of the church as the people of God more than as an impersonal bureaucracy. How else do Catholics, Christians, non-Christians, and even atheists encounter the church unless it is through particular individuals? A pope today cannot be held personally responsible for the erroneous and lamentable actions of a pope centuries ago, of course, but certainly the institution of the papacy and the church are burdened by those actions, as John Paul II noted in his homily during the Day of Pardon mass. In addition, some accused John Paul II of propagating a phenomenon that's come to be called "apology chic"— seeking forgiveness because it's politically correct or trendy to do so or in order to quickly get past mistakes—but it's hardly believable that this was John Paul II's motivation.

58. Is the pope the closest person to God on earth?

I heard this question frequently during the spring of 2005 as John Paul II's death and funeral were followed by the preparation for the conclave that elected Benedict XVI. A Philadelphia radio show host related to me that this is what he told his son. This radio host was not pleased when I suggested he should teach his son that he should be the closest person to God on earth, as indeed any believer should. What's behind this question, I suspect, is a caricaturist notion that God and the pope have an instant-access telephone that connects them immediately: God tells the pope what to do and then the pope tells the people what to do.

The pope need not be any more or less holy than your wise grandmother, that good priest who preaches on Sunday, your child, or you. I'm reminded of a story told about Mother Teresa when she was asked, "What's wrong with the church today?" Her response: "Me. I'm what's wrong with the church today, because I'm a sinner." Surely every religious belief, be it Catholic or otherwise, offers the possibility that anyone can be in contact with God at a moment's notice through prayer.

59. Do I have to believe every word the pope says?

Papal infallibility does not mean that every word the pope says is absolutely true and is an article of the Catholic faith that Catholics must believe or otherwise be considered outside the church. While this statement may seem like a straw man—a simplistic description that is easily blown down by the slightest breath of defense or explanation—I am frequently reminded that some version of this statement is really what people still think of when they wonder what papal infallibility means.

Catholic theology teaches that the pope, as a sign of unity, by the authority of his succession to Peter and through his role as bishop of Rome holds in trust those doctrines that make Catholic belief Catholic. He shares this authority with his brother bishops who likewise teach Catholic beliefs throughout the world. There is a difference between dogma and discipline, however. Belief in the Real Presence, a dogma, will not change though our language to describe it could. A discipline, like whether priests in the western church must be celibate, might in fact change. Catholics must obey the pope when he is making those *ex cathedra* statements that are binding on all the faithful. At the same time, the church distinguishes the relative authority of other papal statements in public addresses, interviews, and homilies in addition to formal writings such as encyclicals and apostolic letters. Even among the latter, non-*ex cathedra* statements, however, the church believes Catholics must have a certain deference and submission of the will and intellect—to use the fancier language found in certain church documents—even on matters that have not been pronounced definitively. We should acknowledge, however, that the Vatican is not always clear on the level of authority behind a particular statement or writing. Many would like Vatican teachings to be more specific regarding the authority a particular statement holds, while others are more comfortable with the ambiguity for a variety of reasons. Private opinions, such as what a pope may think of a book, movie, politician, or governmental action are another matter entirely.

B. Cardinals

60. Where do the cardinals come from?

Like the words *pope* and *papacy,* you won't find the word *cardinal* or the phrase *college of cardinals* in the New Testament. But, again like the papacy's growth from authentic roots, the church allows for the natural development of officials and institutions from the early church. This development is the story of the college of cardinals.[39]

There is no direct precedent for the cardinals in scripture, but there was an inner circle around Peter and then his successors as the centuries passed. In the middle of the first millennium, as the Roman Empire collapsed and a papal curia very slowly evolved, priests and deacons staffed about twenty-five or thirty parishes *(tituli)* in the city of Rome, which was surrounded by seven very small dioceses in its suburbs, each headed by a bishop. These three dozen or so bishops, priests, and deacons joined the pope to be collectively called the Roman church. They became the first cardinals, at least in a rudimentary way, and frequently assisted the popes at liturgies and gave them advice on local matters.

As the papacy developed into a medieval monarchy with a larger curia and bureaucracy, it was only natural that these closest advisers similarly evolved into a more formal structure with unique titles, offices, and insignia. Cardinals became ever more important as key players in the Gregorian Revolution we discussed in part I, moving away from their liturgical roles and taking up administrative tasks. Pope Urban II (1088–99) deliberately modeled his curia after English and French royal courts and councils, taking from them examples of how to regulate large property holdings. Cardinals increasingly filled the roles of papal ambassadors or legates and gathered around the pope as a group of advisers—something like a cabinet. They led curial departments and sometimes appeared in medieval and modern church documents as heirs to the Roman Senate. The *camerarius* was in charge of finances and the *cancellarius* (chancellor) headed the administrative bureaucracy of documents and records. Four chancellors became pope in the twelfth century alone, indicating that the curia and the office of cardinal quickly were becoming the career path to the papal throne.

During the conciliar challenges and the Great Western Schism of the late Middle Ages, some cardinals asserted that they shared in the power of the papacy—the Latin phrase is *pars corporis papae,* part of the pope's body—while popes countered that bishops and cardinals held power only partially and the pope alone exercised full executive authority. Nevertheless, we see medieval popes signing documents with cardinals as witnesses and stressing that they made decisions *de fratrum nostrum consilio*—with the advice of our brothers. Some cardinals were sent to speak for the pope to recalcitrant bishops, abbots, or secular rulers; they were called papal vicars and were permitted to wear papal symbols and vestments. By the end of the Middle Ages, the cardinals had become a sort of aristocracy or oligarchy sitting between the church's highest level, the papacy, and the layers of bureaucracy below Rome's curia.

61. What do *cardinal* and *college of cardinals* mean?

There is some scholarly debate on the derivation of the word *cardinal*. Two Latin words are the best candidates. The first, *cardo,* means "hinge," indicating the cardinals' role sitting between the church's head (the papacy) and her body (the people of God) as a kind of neck. Like a hinge, the cardinals make the machinery move along properly. This word as the source has fallen out of favor, however, and yielded to *cardinalis,* which indicates that a cardinal is incardinated. This word means that a new cardinal is officially made part of the Roman church, hearkening back to that first group of core advisers in the early church.[40] Even today, strictly speaking, there is no cardinal of Lagos in Nigeria or Seoul in South Korea, for instance; archbishops there, and other cardinal archbishops, hold the formal title of cardinal of the *Roman* church and are assigned a titular (in name only) church in Rome linking them to the city.[41] The word *incardinated* also indicates that, starting in the Middle Ages, a cardinal might be sent from Rome into a new territory to speak in the pope's name and export the idea of a papal authority and monarchy, in which case he is incardinated into a new diocese.[42]

The word *college* comes from the Latin *collegium,* a word used often in the Middle Ages to refer to a group of like-minded people: a guild of tradesmen or business owners, a group of students or professors, or in this case a particular community of church officials. The phrase *college of cardinals* appears more frequently after about 1150. As the Middle Ages progressed, the cardinals met in a consistory, or fairly regular meeting, that gradually replaced occasional synods of bishops as places where popes gathered advice. Within the college, cardinals hold one of three ranks—cardinal bishop, cardinal priest, or cardinal deacon—but these ranks are more reflective of inside ecclesiastical protocol than practical application to parish or diocesan life. Cardinals are members of the college whether they are physically meeting together in a consistory or not, just as bishops share a brotherhood and collegiality regardless of their geographic location.

62. Why do cardinals wear red?

The bright red bird is named after the church's cardinals, not the other way around. The color is brilliant: a burnt orange-red referred to as scarlet. Red symbolizes the cardinal's willingness to die for the faith. This meaning is inserted into the ceremony during which a cardinal wears his red robes for the first time. As the pope invests the new cardinal with his red hat, he says: "[This is] red as a sign of the dignity of the cardinal, meaning that you must be ready to behave with courage, up to the shedding of blood, for the increase of the Christian faith, for the peace and tranquility of the People of God, and for the freedom and spreading of the Holy Roman Church."[43] It seems that red became the cardinal's color in the Middle Ages as a sign of distinction; some earlier paintings, frescoes, and manuscripts indicate that blue may have been used in prior centuries to set cardinals or bishops apart.

63. Why do they say someone gets a "red hat" when he's made a cardinal?

Cardinals used to receive three red hats, but now there are only two. The first, and the one used far more than the other, is the little red skullcap, called a zucchetto by those in the know and a beanie by those who aren't. It was originally nothing more than a covering for the cleric's tonsure: a patch of skull shaved of its hair to denote the clergyman's dedication to a life of service. Monks wore black or brown zucchetti.[44] The second hat is the biretta: a stiff cap covered in scarlet silk with four sides and three ridges to form a peak, which is carried more often than worn and which you might see a cardinal holding in his official portrait. The biretta likely evolved as part of the medieval university's robes, hoods, and hats that not only denoted a scholar's rank, but kept him warm in drafty classrooms and libraries.[45] As the church, especially the papacy, continued to borrow from medieval and monastic culture, the biretta and zucchetto were adapted and reserved for ecclesiastical ranks with different colors and shapes.[46]

The third hat of former times was a broad-brimmed galero that looks somewhat like a stiff sombrero. The galero was left aside in 1969 as part of a post-Vatican II downsizing of church pageantry. In practice (after the Middle Ages when it was a reasonable size), the galero was never really worn because it was huge—think of a round kitchen table for a breakfast nook. During the consistory, the galero was held over the new cardinal's head, then often carried in procession the first time he returned to his home cathedral. Look up at a cathedral that was home to a cardinal and you will probably see the galero suspended over a crypt or tomb where cardinals are buried. After their deaths, the cardinals' galeros are hoisted up to hang from the ceiling, draped by many tassels that signify their particular titles and ranks.

64. I heard that the number of cardinals who elect the pope is limited, but there seem to be so many more of them now. Were there always so many?

For more than half of the church's life, there were very few cardinals in the college. We have accounts of just a handful or less than twenty cardinals gathering to elect a pope. As the medieval papacy expanded the role and use of the college of cardinals, the number rose. Popes made three hundred cardinals throughout the twelfth century and another 140 in the thirteenth century, although at any one time there were only a few dozen; life spans being shorter in the Middle Ages, there was a high turnover in the college. Church councils in the fifteenth century set twenty-four as the number of cardinals in the college, but there was some discussion that forty might be a better figure. Pope Sixtus V (1585–90) established a limit of seventy cardinals for the college, perhaps using the example of Moses' group of seventy elders as advisers (Num 11:16), but in practical terms Sixtus probably raised the number so substantially in order to decrease the power of any individual cardinal. In any event, this full complement of seventy was rarely reached in the following centuries.

Closer to our own times, John XXIII (1958–63), never a man bound by tradition, saw the number seventy as impractical for the modern world; after he named cardinals, there were eighty-seven by 1962. Paul VI (1963–78) stipulated than once a cardinal turned eighty years old, he could not enter a conclave to vote for a pope, setting 120 as the number of cardinal electors. John Paul II, yet another pope who did not bow to precedent, reaffirmed his predecessor's limit and then simply ignored it. John Paul II's college held as many as 185 cardinals with more than 120 electors—up to 135 at one point.[47] To give another sense of the unprecedented growth of the college in the last half century: fifty-one cardinals elected John XXIII in 1958, then just five years later eighty cardinals elected Paul VI, while 111 elected John Paul II in 1978 and 115 elected Benedict XVI in 2005.

Apart from the number of cardinals, a distinguishing characteristic of the modern college is its relative geographic diversity.[48] Since the Middle Ages, both the papacy and the college of cardinals were sometimes dominated by Italians and politics. When the medieval popes fought Holy Roman emperors in central Europe, they rarely named German cardinals. During the Avignon papacy in the fourteenth century, nearly every cardinal was French. As early as the twelfth century, Bernard of Clairvaux (1090–1153) advised his former student Eugene III (1145–53) to name cardinals from all over Christian territory—at that time, meaning the limits of Europe—because the faith was spreading and their decisions would affect more than just Italian Christians. It was Paul VI who made the college ever more international to reflect a growing church that, because it was truly global, was indeed "catholic" or universal in a manner impossible for much of the church's prior life. Together, Paul VI and John Paul II especially named cardinals from emerging countries and places where Catholicism is growing: Africa, southeast Asia, eastern Europe, and Latin America.

Today, cardinals from the so-called third or developing world make up about a third of the college.

65. Are all cardinals bishops?

Almost every single one, with notable exceptions. Current canon law stipulates that all cardinals are supposed to be bishops, which is what John XXIII had declared in 1962. If a priest who is not yet a bishop is named a cardinal, he is supposed to be ordained bishop. Pragmatically, on the rare occasions when a pope names a priest who is not a bishop to the college of cardinals, the pope will leave it up to that new cardinal to decide if he wishes to be ordained a bishop. Typically, the priest is a leading theologian, already older than eighty, and ineligible to vote in conclave. He usually asks the pope to overlook the requirement that he be ordained a bishop, a request the pope then grants. To give a few examples from the papacy of John Paul II, this happened in 1983 with the eighty-seven-year-old French Jesuit Henri de Lubac, in 1988 with the eighty-two-year-old Swiss theologian Hans Urs von Balthasar (who died two days before he was to receive his red hat), and in 2001 with the Jesuit theologian Avery Dulles, eighty-two, of Fordham University. Similarly, when Benedict XVI named the eighty-two-year-old French Jesuit Albert Vanhoye a cardinal in 2006, he granted the scripture scholar's request that he not be ordained a bishop. Though such cardinals are not bishops, they still are entitled to wear a miter, ring, and pectoral cross. Because they are not bishops, however, they cannot do some of things that only bishops can, like ordain men deacons, priests, or bishops.

66. Is it true that if the pope wanted to appoint a woman to be a cardinal, he could?

No. You might have heard the saying that only God could create the world and only popes can create cardinals. This is true, but popes are bound by canon law and the same rule that stipulates cardinals must be bishops also refers to cardinals as men who are priests:

"Those to be promoted Cardinals are men freely selected by the Roman Pontiff, who are at least in the order of the priesthood...."[49] Now, it is also true that we have just seen examples where the pope dispensed the rule that cardinals must be bishops. It is highly unlikely, however, that a pope would go a much bigger step forward and dispense from the rule that a priest be a man. The explanation most commonly heard is that the law saying cardinals should be bishops is a human law, which a pope can change, but that the law saying a priest must be male is a divine law, which a pope cannot change.

For trivia buffs: the last layman made a cardinal was an Italian jurist, Teodolfo Mertel, who wrote laws governing the papal territories. Pope Pius IX made him a cardinal in 1858; he was ordained a deacon two months later.

67. Has there ever been a pope elected who wasn't a cardinal?

Technically speaking, the person elected pope need be only a baptized male. If the man selected is not a bishop or a priest, he must immediately be ordained a priest and then a bishop. At the moment of his episcopal ordination, he becomes pope. The last cardinal who was not already a bishop to be elected pope was Bartolomeo Cappellari, who became Pope Gregory XVI (1831–46). Already a priest, he was ordained a bishop four days after his election as pope.

During the church's first millennium, before the college of cardinals was formalized during the Gregorian Revolution, some non-cardinals were elected pope. During the Middle Ages, the trend toward selecting a pope from among the cardinal electors became the norm. The last time a non-cardinal was elected pope was in 1378, an event we have already discussed in part I. That was the year a deadlocked conclave of sixteen cardinals, most of them French wanting to return to Avignon, reached outside the conclave and elected an Italian archbishop as Urban VI (1378–89). This contentious election, followed by Urban's unstable behavior, the

French cardinals' renunciation of their election of him, and their subsequent election of a rival pope led to the nearly forty-year Great Western Schism. Given this history, it is not surprising that the cardinals have not gone outside the college to elect a pope since 1378.

C. Papal Death and Succession

68. What happens when a pope dies?

There is no surprise about what happens when a pope dies. A papal death is the starting pistol for a well-defined set of events that occurs in precise order, with only the details being left to circumstance or a particular pope's final directions about his own funeral and burial.

First, the pope's death must be certified. The traditional little silver hammer used to tap the man's head while his baptismal name is called out three times—followed by the statement, "You are dead"—has been replaced by medical equipment. Second, the papal apartments are sealed: the doors are locked while phone and fax lines are cut until the next pope takes possession of his new home. Third, a series of what are essentially wakes are held: John Paul II's body was first laid out in a large Vatican hall for diplomats, prelates, and other dignitaries before it was moved to St. Peter's Basilica for hours of nonstop lines of mourners to pass.

A pope's funeral must be celebrated and he must be buried within four to six days after his death. He may have left instructions as to who he would like to preach or what music might be played, not unlike anyone else who plans his or her own funeral. Paul VI wanted a simple coffin and an open book of the gospels laid on top, an arrangement that John Paul II replicated. During his papacy, John Paul II had thought about being buried in his native Poland. His body was eventually interred below the Vatican, along with the bodies of other popes, and was placed in a series of caskets: first cypress, then zinc, and finally walnut. A pope is also typically buried with a record of his writings and the major events of his life and papacy. After the funeral and burial, a nine-day period of mourning follows called the *novemdiales*. The conclave must begin fifteen to twenty days after the death. When a pope's death is announced, therefore, it is usually just under three weeks before the conclave is held.

69. Who's in charge between popes?

The period between popes is called an interregnum, meaning "between the reigns." We say that the chair of St. Peter is vacant during this time—the Latin phrase is *sede vacante*. In the interval, the ordinary running of the church falls to the college of cardinals. They act as caretakers, but can't do certain things that only the pope can, such as call a general council, name bishops, and promulgate doctrinal statements. The cardinals meet frequently between the papal death and the conclave, at first setting the timetable and details of the papal funeral and burial. They oversee the funeral and burial, see to it that the papal ring is destroyed—a throwback to the time when a ring's face was a seal used to authenticate documents—and prepare for the conclave. The cardinals are led by their dean and some key Vatican officials. The *camerlengo* is another busy person during the interregnum; he is something like a president or prime minister's chief of staff. He is in charge of many of the details and timetables laid down by the college of cardinals.

70. What's a conclave?

A conclave is the closed-door meeting at which the cardinals younger than eighty years old, and therefore eligible to vote, select a successor to the recently deceased pope.[50] The word derives from the Latin phrase *cum clave* (with a key); it came, by way of Latin and Italian, into English as conclave. The cardinals are to be kept apart from outside interference by voluntarily walking into this locked room and staying there until they elect a pope. In 1903, one cardinal sent ripples of laughter through his colleagues when he noted aloud they were entering the sealed conclave on the eve of the feast of St. Peter in chains.

Today, the conclave's locked room is the Vatican's Sistine Chapel, commissioned by Pope Sixtus IV (1471–84). A dominant and appropriate fresco there is *Christ Consigns the Keys to Peter* by Pietro Perugino, depicting the scene of Matthew 16:19—Jesus giving the keys to Peter. The Sistine Chapel's ceiling contains Michelangelo's famous sixteenth-century fresco of the Creation, highlighted by God and Adam touching fingertips, and his *Last Judgement,* painted several decades later, above the altar.

The conclave is to have the nature of a sacred retreat, according to the conclave regulations put into place by Pope Paul VI in 1975.[51] In 1978, England's Cardinal Basil Hume noted he became strongly aware that in the conclave, there is "nothing between the cardinals and God."[52] John Paul II, in his own conclave instructions issued in 1996, reminded the cardinals that they will sit under the *Last Judgement,* making the place "conducive to an awareness of the presence of God, in whose sight each person will one day be judged."[53]

The cardinals sit in the Sistine Chapel to vote twice each day; each session has two ballots, although the opening evening session, after a Mass and many procedural matters, can have just one ballot. No electioneering, nomination speeches, or other types of politicking are to occur in the Chapel. All they do during these two sessions is vote. Each cardinal has a few preprinted ballots with the words *Eligo in Summum Pontificem*—"I elect as Supreme Pontiff"— and then a blank line. Disguising their handwriting, they write one name, fold the paper, and then each in turn walks through the main aisle holding the ballot so all can see. They place the ballot in an urn (formerly a large chalice when there were just a few dozen ballots) sitting on the altar and return to their seats after declaring aloud, "I call as my witness Christ the Lord who will be my judge, that my vote is given to the one who before God I think should be elected." Several cardinals chosen by lot, and changed every few ballots, count the papers. If the number of unopened ballots does not match the number of cardinals, they are burned without being opened or counted. If the numbers match, they are read (or scrutinized, to use the official phrase) by one cardinal who makes a tally silently, then by another who does the same, then by a third who reads the name aloud. This last cardinal passes a needle and thread through the word *Eligo* to mark that the ballot has been counted once, canceling it out like a train ticket that has been punched and can't be used again. If no cardinal reaches the required two-thirds majority, or two-thirds plus one if the number of cardinals in the chapel is not divisible by three, the ballots are burned and another vote takes place if two have not occurred. Otherwise, the cardinals break for lunch or quit for the day. If a candidate does reach the required number, he is asked two questions: Does he accept and by what name will he be known? As soon as he accepts, he is pope.

Strictly speaking, as soon as the man has accepted election, the conclave is concluded, although some time passes before the door seals are broken and the news is announced officially. First, the new pope must be vested in a side chapel prosaically called the Chapel of Tears. None of the vestments fit the portly John XXIII in 1958; the biggest cassock had to be pulled, tucked, torn, pinned, and hidden under a surplice. "I feel trussed up and ready for delivery," he declared.[54] Then, upon returning to the Sistine Chapel, the new pope receives the congratulations of the cardinals. According to a cardinal from Cologne, Pope John Paul I told them in 1978, "God will forgive you for what you have done to me."[55] Meanwhile, the burned ballots are supposed to give off white smoke (thanks to a chemical pellet) to indicate a successful election or black smoke if no candidate received the necessary number of votes. Bells ring and, in today's wired world, cell phones and beepers go off. Within an hour or so, the cardinals appear on the balcony and one makes the traditional announcement: *Habemus papam*—"We have a pope!" His given name is then announced, followed by his papal name. The new pope steps forward, speaks briefly, and then gives his first public blessing.

71. Was this always the way to elect a pope?

No. The conclave is not even half as old as the church her-self—less than a thousand years—and dates to the Middle Ages. For about a thousand years, it seems that bishops of Rome were selected in different ways. At first, when Christianity was still an outlawed religion, the successors to Peter were probably simply the obvious choice among a very small circle of brave leaders in the city of Rome. It may have been that a sitting bishop had indicated who he thought would be the right man to follow, but this was no worldly honor and certainly not one without danger. Many of the first bishops of Rome probably died for the faith, although the records are very scanty indeed. One account of an election in 236 notes that a dove settled on the head of Fabian, a Christian who was not even mentioned among several candidates. Fabian was chosen because the dove was interpreted as a sign of the Holy Spirit's choice.

After the Roman emperors made Christianity the official and only religion of the empire in the late fourth century, successors to Peter came from the ranks of Roman Christians who had experi-ence in imperial administration. The sources often say that the Roman people, the Roman church, the Roman clergy, or some combination of these groups selected their own bishop. This prob-ably means that the natural leaders of the clergy settled on a man, but that the laity—sometimes including the emperor—weighed in on the choice. Over time, this offering of an opinion probably took the form of a man being selected by the leading clerics and secu-lar officials at a gathering. They then probably led him out to a waiting crowd of Christians who "acclaimed" him by shouting out their acceptance.

By about the middle of the eighth century, it seems that more formality was coming into play. An Italian synod in 769 declared that all of the Roman clerics could vote, but that only the cardinals—the heads of those *tituli* or urban parishes—were in the pool of candi-dates. Once chosen, the man would have to be acclaimed by the crowd and, at times, accepted by the emperor. Before long, how-ever, and certainly around the end of the first millennium and the beginning of the second, the Roman aristocracy was controlling the election, putting their favored sons and brothers on the papal throne with diminishing concern for the man's theological train-ing, administrative skill, pastoral zeal, or spirituality.[56]

72. Sounds messy. Is that why the procedures were changed?

In the long run, yes: the selection of the pope had to be free from outside control. The papal election, therefore, must be seen in the context of the Gregorian Revolution and its goal of *libertas ecclesiae*—the freedom of the church to name her own leaders, police her own ranks, and declare her own doctrine and discipline. If the popes wanted bishops and abbots to be chosen without sec-ular control, it became important that the popes be elected freely, as well. In fact, it was critical: the papal election had to be the best example of an independent election at the top of the hierarchy in order for freedom to be permitted and imitated throughout the rest of the church's levels. In a sense, the Gregorian popes were try-ing to make sure that the investiture controversies we discussed in part I no longer interfered with papal elections, which is what had been occurring.[57]

To achieve this goal, the popes designated the cardinals as the right group of people to handle the papal election. In 1059, Pope Nicholas II declared the cardinals were to have the leading voice in the papal election rather than the Roman aristocracy, although the regulations still allowed the rest of the Roman clergy to par-ticipate and permitted the sitting pope to indicate, though not appoint, his choice for successor. A general council called Lateran III in 1179 formally restricted the election's voting to just the car-dinals: from that time on, the cardinals became the exclusive elec-tors for pope. Because a small number of cardinals could produce deadlocks easily, Lateran III also broke the long-standing requirement of a unanimous vote. From then on, the one who receives two-thirds of the cardinals' votes is the validly elected pope.

73. Who created the conclave?

Despite the changes made by Nicholas II and Lateran III, the church still didn't have its conclave. Every long-simmering problem requires a flashpoint to bring the issue together and demand a resolution. The flashpoint followed the death of Pope Clement IV in 1268 in the Italian city of Viterbo. Rules at the time stipulated that the election of a pope must take place in the city where the prior pope had died. This arrangement made great sense because, at the time, when the pope traveled the small number of cardinals making up the college at that time typically accompanied him. With no method of long-distance communication, when a pope left Rome, the administrative apparatus went with him. So most of the cardinals were not in Rome or home dioceses, but right there with the pope.

This time, however, the cardinals didn't simply sit down and decide. They started, but German, Italian, and French rulers were trying particularly hard to influence this election. The cardinals themselves were unusually divided and for a year spent as much time wandering through Viterbo as gathering to vote. Viterbo's city officials decided to force a decision: they gathered the cardinals into a hall, locked the doors, and demanded the college pick a pope. When the cardinals even then failed to choose, the officials ripped the roof off the hall, exposing the cardinals to the sun and rain, and warned them that their food would be cut off next. Two cardinals died and another became so sick he had to leave. The roof was restored, but still no pope was chosen. Under enormous pressure from inside as well as outside the church, the cardinals picked a subcommittee, agreed to accept its choice, and waited until six of them settled on a man who was not even present and who was neither priest, bishop, nor cardinal. Even though he was far away in the Holy Land, this man eventually became Gregory X, though he didn't make it to Viterbo until February 1272, almost six months after his election, and wasn't ordained for another six weeks.

Gregory X (1271–76), a very capable pope, wanted to insure that the circumstances of his own election were never repeated. Under his leadership, a general council called Lyons II in 1274 formalized the Viterbo experience. Lyons II gave the church her conclave, stipulating that the cardinals were to meet within ten days after the pope died in the city where he had passed away. They would be locked up with a key and could choose a pope by three methods: scrutiny (casting votes in the traditional manner), acclamation (they all agree easily on a man through a voice vote), or delegation (a subcommittee makes a choice that all the other cardinals agree in advance to accept). If there was no pope after three days, then the cardinals' two meals per day would be restricted to one course only. If eight days passed without a selection, the cardinals received only bread, water, and wine. Moreover, to provide a more worldly incentive for a quick election, the rules stipulated that the cardinals could not receive any money from the papal treasury without a living pope. While elections after Lyons II did sometimes go on for quite some time—months, even—these regulations have largely guided conclaves since then.

74. Have conclaves changed over the centuries?

Not much. The history of papal conclaves since Lyons II represents logical adaptations to that council's rules, but nothing that changes their goal of a free, fair, protected, and quick election.

In 1621, Pope Gregory XV made several changes to try to speed things up. He declared that the ballot would be secret: no cardinal had to make his choice known and so written ballots came to be more the norm than a voice or hand vote. On that ballot, cardinals were to list only one name and not several, as had been the procedure. With a multiname ballot, a cardinal might be the tenth choice—the bottom of the list—but if he appeared on everyone's ballot, he might be elected pope because the number of times a name appeared and not the order counted. Someone else who might be in the top three could have enemies—as front-runners or standouts in any field or election often do—and therefore not appear on every single ballot. Such a process almost guarantees a mediocre selection. Furthermore, the cardinals were to disguise their handwriting when putting down their choice, adding another layer of privacy, and they weren't supposed to vote for themselves. Gregory XV also abolished acclamation as one of the three choices: a vote had to take place, be it by the whole college or a subcommittee. Finally, Gregory XV doubled the number of votes each day to two from one, which had been customary, again in order to hasten a choice.

After Lyons II and Gregory XV, conclave rules remained basically the same until very recently. All conclaves now take place in Rome, regardless of where the pope might die; the last conclave away from Rome was in Venice in 1800. As mentioned earlier, the conclave must begin between fifteen and twenty days after the pope's death: no earlier and no later. If a cardinal does not arrive in time, he may now enter after the conclave doors are sealed shut, but this was not always the rule. When the ten-day rule was in effect before the jet age, cardinals sometimes did not make it in time for the conclave and were shut out. Today, a cardinal far away from Rome, such as a remote area of Australia, can usually make it to the city within forty-eight hours, but this was not always the case. Some colorful American stories can stand for those of cardinals from other parts of the world. John McCloskey, archbishop of New York, was the first American made a cardinal, but he missed the 1878 election that chose Leo XIII. The first American cardinal to vote was Baltimore's James Gibbons in 1903 because he was in Rome on other business. He and Boston's William O'Connell missed the next election, in 1914. Sailing to Rome on the fastest ship they could find, they landed in Naples and had a driver race to Rome, only to hear the bells announcing the election of Benedict XV in the distance. Determined to be ready next time, Cardinal O'Connell made arrangements beforehand: he flew from Boston to New York to a ship that was held at the dock just for him. Landing at the port of Naples, he jumped on a reserved train to Rome. Arriving in Rome and running through the streets, he again heard the bells signaling election, this time of Pius XII. The cardinal told the new pope, reportedly vociferously, that more time was needed. Pius XII agreed and changed the amount of time between the papal death and the conclave to fifteen days and allowed an extension to twenty days if necessary.[58]

Popes of the late twentieth century dramatically increased the number of cardinals while Paul VI restricted the electors to those cardinals under the age of eighty. John Paul II in 1996 made some substantive changes, but again these are adaptations to the modern world and the larger size of the college, not radical departures from tradition. Because of the large number of electors now, for instance, the cardinals deposit their ballots into urns instead of the chalice of prior centuries because a chalice cannot hold more than a hundred ballots. John Paul II reasserted that only a written vote was valid, repeating Gregory XV's prohibition of acclamation, but further removing the option of delegation whereby a subcommittee decided for the whole college. In the event of a long conclave, John Paul II allowed for some pauses and changes to the number of votes required for election. Three days without an election can be followed by a break of up to a day; this process can be repeated after seven more fruitless ballots. If eight days go by without a pope, the cardinals can discuss what to do next. One option is to restrict their votes to the top two vote-getters in the most recent ballot. If twelve days pass without a pope, the two-thirds rule can be suspended and a man can be elected with 50 percent of the vote plus one, but Benedict XVI restored the two-thirds rule in 2007.

The most significant change John Paul II made was in the living arrangements. Certainly these received the most media attention when his conclave rules were released in 1996 and then again in 2005 when they were implemented for the first time. But only romantics and impractical traditionalists would deny the need to bring the process up to date. John Paul II realized that having more than one hundred elderly men sleep on cots separated by curtains, cram into tiny rooms off the Sistine Chapel, and share toilets just was not practical and no longer made sense. He had a dormitory built especially for the conclaves, the *Domus Sanctae Martae* (House of St. Martha, named after Jesus' friend), which would normally be used by Vatican visitors. Most are single rooms, with a few double-room suites, all assigned by lot; there is a common eating area, chapels, and private bathrooms. During the conclave, the cardinals are shuttled back and forth from the *Domus* to the Sistine Chapel twice each day like a sequestered jury. One change that the cardinals themselves decided in the days leading up to the 2005 conclave was that they could walk in the Vatican gardens when they weren't voting, though they were still to be isolated from everyone but each other. Because of modern technology, the rules also stipulate that the cardinals can have no contact with anyone outside: personal contact is excluded, of course, but there are also no cell phones, beepers, pagers, faxes, telephones, newspapers, magazines, e-mail or Internet access, radio or television.

75. We keep hearing about oaths of secrecy, closed doors, and white smoke. It sounds very cloak-and-dagger. Were things always so secretive?

We must make a critical distinction between *secrecy* and *confidentiality*. Use the word *secrecy* and suddenly the conversation seems to be about backdoor deals and things the cardinals don't want anyone else to learn. But change the word to *confidentiality* and then we find ourselves in more familiar territory. There are many areas of confidentiality that we consider comfortable, essential, and even indispensable: between an attorney or a counselor and a client, doctors and patients, husbands and wives, friends, priests and penitents, and ministers or rabbis and their congregants. We find nothing wrong with confidentiality when it comes to a sequestered jury deciding the guilt of a defendant; we talk so much and so openly about politics that we forget the western system of constitutionalism and democracy is based on a private ballot. After all the drama, grief, news coverage, travel, busy-ness of a papal funeral and conclave preparations, it makes sense for the college of cardinals to take a collective breath and to enter the sacred retreat of the conclave in silence and prayer. To make the decision, they need quiet and they need to be away from distractions. Having a camera in the Sistine Chapel would invade the experience; think of how televised trials are affected merely because a camera is in the courtroom.

No one is naïve enough to think that there isn't politics involved in the conclave; of course there is. The cardinals are human beings, after all, and some may be driven by ambition. But just because some past elections were engineered by camps of cardinals and secular rulers doesn't mean today's conclaves must be bound by that troublesome past. Indeed, the rules explicitly forbid politicking to take place in the conclave proper, that is, during the voting in the Sistine Chapel. Many cardinals, like many jurors, have noted how they genuinely felt the burden of their task when the doors are closed and the decision is before them. Casting about for groups or cliques and taking the pulse of the direction in which support will be offered or withheld likely occurs at meals and meetings, not in the Sistine Chapel. After a lengthy papacy, especially, cardinals have been meeting in Rome and around the world, although admittedly the large number of them makes personal contact with everyone nearly impossible. At some consistories, cardinals have worn the equivalent of fancy "Hello, my name is…" tags on their bright red robes. Plenty of politics has been done already; opinions have already been formed.

We should note, too, that part of the reason for confidentiality and protection of the voting process dates back to the many centuries of interference by secular rulers.[59] For centuries, emperors claimed to have the right to veto papal candidates, though this extreme example of interference is difficult to prove. The last and relatively recent example often cited occurred in the 1903 election when the Austrians declared they would not accept the Vatican secretary of state because he was allegedly too pro-French.[60] Medieval history also provides examples of the papacy and elections being tainted by secular interference. Viewed in this long light of history, confidentiality makes a great deal of sense.

During the meetings before the conclave, the cardinals promise several times to follow the election rules and to keep confidentiality; cardinals over the age of eighty are permitted to participate in these preconclave meetings, although they cannot vote in the election itself. Anyone locked in with the cardinals must also take an oath to keep what they see and hear confidential forever, on pain of excommunication, unless explicitly permitted to speak by a subsequent pope. Conclaves used to be crowded with the cardinals' personal staffs: most brought an entourage of cook, doctor, priest-secretary, confessor, housekeeper, laundress, and others. Now the number is strictly restricted to just a shared handful of canon lawyers, doctors, staffers to handle paperwork and technical issues, and liturgical assistants. Anyone else is dismissed with the traditional call of *extra omnes*—"everybody else out"! In 1922, a reporter was discovered as a stowaway of sorts—he'd tried to switch places with a waiter—and a photographer was found hiding, too. Electronic sweeps now take place to discover bugs, but today's advanced technology must mean that someone is surely trying to listen in from afar with satellite dishes or other high-tech spy gear.

With the relocation of the cardinals' physical needs to the *Domus Sanctae Martae,* it may be more difficult for such staffers to hear what is going on inside the Sistine Chapel, although afterward scholars, reporters, and Vatican insiders often try to get cardinals to speak off the record or to glean from what staffers overheard and saw to reconstruct votes. It was not always difficult. During the conclave of 1549–50, the Holy Roman Emperor Charles V allegedly knew when the cardinals visited their chamberpots. Medieval and Renaissance bookies got their information from names and vote tallies chalked onto the bottom of dirty dishes passed from the conclave to the outside world's kitchen. A leading scholar of papal conclaves, Frederic Baumgartner, notes that the

obsession with secrecy or confidentiality is largely a modern phenomenon dating back only about one hundred and fifty years. In
compiling his history of the conclaves, he was able to reconstruct
many of the conclaves' tallies from 1600 to 1846 from existing
records. Today, all of the cardinals' notes are burned; one record of
the votes is placed in a sealed envelope and stored in the Vatican
Archives, but it is not accessible to anyone without the pope's permission. The white smoke signaling an election that some think has
a long history seems a fairly recent phenomenon, too, and is connected with the burning of the ballots, making the white smoke a
tradition of maybe only a century.[61]

76. What were the shortest and longest conclaves?

Since 1846, conclaves have been short: less than a week and
even just one or two days. The longest conclave was that Viterbo
event, lasting two years and nine months between 1268 and 1271,
making that the longest period without a pope in church history.
The last long conclaves were in 1740, which lasted about six
months, and in 1830 to 1831, which went on for fifty-four days or
nearly eight weeks.

77. Is it true that when a pope has a long reign and names many cardinals, the next pope is just like him?

The Italians have an expression: fat pope, skinny pope. This
indicates that popes who follow each other are usually very different. Almost comically, this expression is physically true at times.
The heavy-set Pius IX was followed in 1878 by a lanky Leo XIII;
in the twentieth century, the gaunt Pius XII was succeeded by the
jolly and jowly John XXIII in 1958, himself succeeded by the thin
and reticent Paul VI in 1963. But caricatures aside, this question
hearkens back to the different types of popes the church has had
for the last century and a half. In fact, a close look at history dis-

covers that when a pope has reigned for a long time, he is followed by a man who can be different in significant ways even though the long-reigning pope named many, if not most, of the college of cardinals.

Let's be more specific. Pius IX reigned thirty-two years and his successor Leo XIII's papacy lasted twenty-five years. We have already noted that Pius IX's distrust of modernity was curtailed somewhat by Leo XIII's turning of the church toward a more activist faith involved in daily affairs. Leo was fairly open to modern scholarship, but his successor Pius X fought modernism bitterly. Closer to our own time, John Paul II (1978–2005) reigned so long and with such a dominant personality that at the time of his death people spoke of the "John Paul generation": young people who knew no other pope in their lifetime. John Paul II named so many cardinals because he wanted a large and diverse college, yes, but also simply because his reign was so long that, late in his life, he named successors to bishops and cardinals he had appointed in his first decade as pope. John Paul II had named 113 of the 115 cardinals who elected his successor. Only two cardinals who participated in the 2005 election had been around for the 1978 conclaves: the United States' William Baum and Germany's Joseph Ratzinger. After his death, there was much talk that John Paul II's successor would be a John Paul Jr. or literally a John Paul III. We cannot fully compare John Paul II with Benedict XVI yet, but clearly they had different approaches to certain topics such as interreligious dialogue. So, yes, there can be striking comparisons in style and substance from one pope—even a long-serving one who almost entirely replaced the college of cardinals—to the next, but this fact is also true of companies, universities, and countries. New leaders have their own agendas and bring in their own inner circles. They emphasize and deemphasize certain issues based on their own skills, priorities, and the context in which they live and serve—a context that might be quite different from that of a predecessor and therefore require a quite different response.

A saying related to this question is, "Whoever goes into a conclave as a pope comes out as a cardinal." A cardinal who looks like he's on the short list to be a pope is called *papabile*—"pope-able." Some of these men are elected and others are not, making the phrase, which used to be true, not very accurate for recent elections. Joseph Ratzinger was a startling choice in 2005, but only because he was so obvious everyone overlooked him. In 1958, Angelo Roncalli may have been the surprise John XXIII to the world, but not to insiders because he fit a certain bill: an older fellow with broad diplomatic experience needed for the Cold War and arms race, plus a bright personality to follow the long and difficult reign of Pius XII. Giovanni Montini went into the 1963 conclave as pope and came out just that way, as Paul VI. Some had their eyes on Albino Luciani going into the 1978 election. When John Paul I's papacy ended suddenly after a month, the cardinals reportedly returned to an athletic candidate who apparently enjoyed emerging support in the earlier conclave that year: Poland's Karol Wojtyla.

78. What happens if a pope becomes incapacitated and can't serve as pope anymore?

As John Paul II aged and became debilitated right before the world's eyes, many asked this question. In his case, it appeared that his body failed while his mind remained sharp, although it is hard to know precisely what was occurring during his final days and a certain amount of privacy must be respected even for such a public figure. But his private state is linked with the public institution of the church. Certainly a media-driven, information-hungry age such as ours will no longer tolerate the way things used to proceed in the Vatican when it was commonly said that a pope was not sick until he was dead.

Unlike modern governments that have succession procedures, such as in the United States, which has the 25th Amendment to the Constitution, the church has no such policy. In this age of advanced medical science, there is a very real possibility that a man could be mentally incapacitated, such as being "brain dead," but still alive. At this point in a family's life, the next questions deal with health care proxies, living wills, and the like, but the papacy has no such next steps laid out or, at least, they have not been made public. So, while this is an excellent question, it is also an extremely troubling one because there is no answer. The lack of such a process is a major problem for the church and one that nearly everyone agrees must be addressed.[62] What if a pope, healthy when elected, developed Alzheimer's disease? In that case, he could not resign because canon law (canon 187) stipulates a person must be of sound mind to resign.

It may be, however, that a foresighted pope could write a will or make a statement indicating what should happen if such an incapacitating circumstance befell him, although there is some disagreement even here. A number of canon lawyers and theologians wonder if an undated letter could be declared valid: even if the pope is of sound mind when the letter was signed, he might not be when the letter becomes valid by being dated. A pope could become suddenly incapacitated because of an accident, a medical condition, a stroke, an emotional or mental breakdown, or even a physical attack like an assassination attempt. In these cases, a document written beforehand or an unexpected catastrophic event, one imagines that the college of cardinals, perhaps led by the *camerlengo* or the college's dean, would play a leading role because they already are assigned this responsibility and duty during the *sede vacante* between a pope's death and the conclave. Of course, it might also be true that a pope may seem fine to himself but not to be judged capable by others, such as the *camerlengo* or the cardinals. In this case, the church could be at a seemingly hopeless impasse because of that ancient dictum that the pope may be judged by no one.

79. Have popes resigned or been deposed?

We have already seen in part I that popes were deposed by emperors and church councils. A handful of popes resigned, too, mostly in the church's first millennium. The first had been Pontian

(230–35), who stepped down when he was deported from Rome during an imperial persecution. He was sent to a prison on the island of Sardinia that was known to be so brutal that everyone died there, so Pontian seemed to want to be sure that the Christian community in Rome would not be without a leader. It is an enduring error to say that the last pope to resign was Celestine V in 1294. The error probably persists because Dante Alighieri (1265–1321), in his *Inferno,* famously placed Celestine V just inside the gate of hell for his "great refusal" *(il gran rifiuto)* of the papal office due to cowardice.[63]

In fact, the last time papal depositions and resignations occurred was during the Great Western Schism of the late fourteenth and early fifteenth centuries when three papal lines competed. Gregory XII (1406–15) of the Roman line issued his resignation at the Council of Constance through his delegates there, but only after calling the already-assembled council into session under his authority, thereby legitimating any actions it might take in electing a successor and, according to some interpretations, leaving unbroken the line of succession down from Peter. The council deposed the other two popes: Benedict XIII of the Avignon line and John XXIII of the Pisan or conciliar line.

There is nothing to stop a pope from resigning: according to canon law, the resignation must be made freely and openly, but it does not have to be accepted by anyone. At first glance, this last part might seem odd, but we can fairly ask: Who would receive a papal resignation? As with the issue of papal incapacitation, one imagines that the *camerlengo,* the college of cardinals or its dean, or perhaps the pope's vicar for the diocese of Rome would play a role in the case of a papal resignation, but nothing is set in policy on this question. Pius XII reportedly had among his papers an undated letter of resignation that would go into effect if Vatican City were to be invaded by the forces of Hitler or Mussolini during World War II. Paul VI, on whom the office of the papacy weighed heavily, was also said to have considered stepping down.

As for the related issue of retirement, in 1966, Paul VI set the mandatory retirement age for bishops at seventy-five, although there is a little leeway: bishops must submit their resignations around their seventy-fifth birthday, but it is up to the pope to accept the resignation or not. (The resignation is of the bishop's current job or office, not of his status as an ordained bishop: once a bishop, always a bishop.) Paul VI also restricted the election of a pope to cardinals younger than eighty years old, but in neither case did he assign a retirement or resignation age to a pope. Like those who sit on America's Supreme Court, the appointment is for life; unlike the justices, papal retirement or resignation is a rare act, indeed. And even if a papal retirement were to become standardized, there certainly would arise the difficult challenge of how to weigh the actions and statements of a retired pope—pope emeritus?—against those of his sitting successor.

80. We were all shocked when Pope John Paul II was shot. Then, of course, there are all those murder rumors about Pope John Paul I, who died so suddenly after his election. Have any popes been assassinated?

Yes, it is true that popes have been murdered. We might start with Peter, by tradition martyred by being crucified upside down because he did not feel worthy to die as Jesus had. You will always have conspiracy theorists pointing to shady information and rumors, especially during the Renaissance. The period when we know for certain that papal assassination was almost common was that dangerous and turbulent end of the first millennium, which we discussed in part I, when Roman families brutally treated the papacy like their private power source. The papal historian Eamon Duffy painted this period graphically:

> A third of the popes elected between 872 and 1012 died in suspicious circumstances—John VIII (872–82)

bludgeoned to death by his own entourage, Stephen VI
(896–97) strangled, Leo V (903) murdered by his successor Sergius III (904–11), John X (914–28) suffo-
cated, Stephen VIII (939–42) horribly mutilated, a fate
shared by the Greek antipope John XVI (997–98) who,
unfortunately for him, did not die from the removal of
his eyes, nose, lips, tongue and hands.[64]

More recent, though less well known, was an attempt on Paul VI's
life at the Manila airport during his trip to the Philippines in
December 1970. A man dressed as a priest pulled out a foot-long
knife and stabbed in the pope's direction, but a burly Vatican aide
shoved the assailant aside. Paul VI forgave his attacker on the spot.[65]

D. Worldliness

81. When I look at the Vatican, I see a lot of wealth, which doesn't remind me of a poor carpenter named Jesus. Why don't they just stop asking me for money, sell all that artwork, and give it to the poor?

What's often lost in this interesting question is the fact that
the church has a proud tradition of leading the way in helping the
poor through her schools, hospitals, adoption agencies, and many
other relief efforts. True, the Vatican's buildings and the art collec-
tions in its museums often make people wonder if the church is
hoarding valuable objects that she might otherwise sell to give the
money to the poor, in imitation of the advice Jesus gave to rich
people in his day. However, it must be remembered that the church
holds these objects in a kind of trust as an institution that for centuries, especially during the Renaissance years, was a patron and
protector of the arts. More than most countries and other institu-

tions, the church has safeguarded these artworks and made them available to people of all faiths, often at a financial loss because of the massive cost to simply maintain them. To hand off or sell them could well be an act of gross irresponsibility that ignores the church's duty to be a steward of these treasures, many of which are quite literally priceless, even in an age of eBay when people will put a price on anything. How can you put a price on Michelangelo's *Pietà*? As a sculpture done by a specific master in a particular place and time, yes, it can be valued as a piece of art. But as an icon of Western civilization and as a universal symbol of nobility and grief, could anyone even approximate its real value beyond dollars and cents?

Also, an unexpected fact for many people is that the Vatican's finances have often run in the red, not the black. Mismanagement played a role in some of the intrigue surrounding the Vatican Bank in the 1970s and 1980s, even forming a subplot in the movie *The Godfather: Part III*. Not until the early 1990s did the Vatican pull itself out of debt. The Vatican's annual operating budget is about a quarter of a billion dollars, which is relatively small compared to international corporations and the governments of many countries. The money in the Vatican's reserves adds up to about three-quarters of a billion dollars. If you opened the pocketbook and spread this money equally to the world's one billion Roman Catholics, each would receive less than one dollar.[66]

82. It sounds to me like the papacy in the Middle Ages and the Renaissance was often corrupt and greedy. Didn't anyone object at the time?

Yes, people did object, and it is important to see that the sharpest and most valid criticisms came from reformers within the church trying to fix things. Because we're talking about the papacy's worldliness here, it's helpful to listen to two reformers, one medieval and one Renaissance, who tackled this topic.

First, the Cistercian abbot Bernard of Clairvaux (1090–1153) wrote some advice to Pope Eugene III (1145–53) in a treatise called *De consideratione* (see question 64). Bernard pushed Eugene to remember that he was ultimately a shepherd and not a worldly ruler. Right at the time when the papacy was recreating itself as a monarchy, Bernard warned the pope against being sucked into lengthy and convoluted legal cases. You have been elected to serve, not to rule, Bernard told the pope. "Does the throne flatter you? It is a watchtower; from it you oversee everything, exercising not dominion, but ministry through the office of your episcopacy.... Go into [the field of the world] not as a lord, but as a steward." Bernard also reminded Eugene that he was the heir of Peter, who was a simple fisherman and not a courtly king.

> This is Peter, who is known never to have gone in procession adorned with either jewels or silk, covered with gold, carried on a white horse, attended by a knight or surrounded by clamoring servants. But without these trappings, he believed it was enough to be able to fulfill the Lord's command, "If you love me, feed my sheep" (John 21:15). In this finery, you are the successor not of Peter, but of Constantine.

Nevertheless, Bernard did not fail to invoke the two-swords theory and tell Eugene that he was, indeed, higher than secular power.[67]

Another voice of constructive criticism was Erasmus (ca. 1467–1536), who was almost exactly a contemporary of Luther, but who disagreed with Luther on a key point related to the papacy. Luther believed the papacy should not exist because, he claimed, it was not based in scripture, and was corrupt and scandalous at that time. Erasmus admitted the papacy was in bad shape, indeed, but contended at the same time that it was an authentic institution and one worth saving. This feeling did not stop Erasmus from criticizing the papacy in a strong, almost vicious manner.

Erasmus used satire to make his points. One of his works, *Julius Exclusus*, was wisely published anonymously and only after the death of Julius II, who had literally led armies into battle. In it, St. Peter balked at letting Julius into heaven, even though he was pope. Julius tried to talk his way in (unsuccessfully, as it turned out), all the while standing there in armor and not papal robes. In another satire, *The Praise of Folly*, Erasmus repeatedly criticized popes, cardinals, and the curia for worldliness. In passage after passage, he sharply, even snidely, contrasted what the papacy should be with what it had become. I offer but a few samples:

> Our popes, cardinals, and bishops have, for a long while now, diligently followed the example of the state and the practices of the princes, and have come near to beating these nobleman at their own game....As to the supreme pontiffs, if they would recall that they take the place of Christ and would attempt to imitate his poverty, tasks, doctrines, crosses, and disregard of safety; if they were even to contemplate the meaning of the name pope— that is, father—or of the title of most holy, then they would become the most humble and mortified of men....Under the present system what work need be done is handed over to Peter or Paul to do at their leisure, while pomp and pleasure are personally taken care of by the popes...[T]hey believe themselves to be justly called defenders of Christ, bragging that they have routed the enemies of the church—as if the church had any greater enemies than these charlatan popes who encourage the disregard of Christ, who depict him as mercenary, who corrupt his teachings by forced interpretations, and who scandalize him by their infamous lives.[68]

Erasmus' criticisms were rarely heeded, however, and to the end of his life some cardinals wanted to burn him as a heretic while others wanted to give him one of their red hats. Although Erasmus very publicly disagreed with Luther, some Catholics declared that Luther hatched the egg that Erasmus had laid.

83. What were the papal states?

The papal states were made up of a swath of land in central Italy. While the borders changed over time, the area always included Rome and generally ran in a northeast pattern across the boot of Italy. It appears, as we saw already in part I, that Constantine in the early fourth century and Pepin in the middle of the eighth century provided land to the popes to give them a ring of physical safety, protection, and income. But the states were also a burden: they encumbered the papacy by making the pope a secular ruler as well as a spiritual one. His decisions had to take into account the material well-being of his territory, which might sometimes influence and even distract his judgment on spiritual matters and alliances with other rulers. Medieval emperors often had their eye on controlling the papal states as a way of squeezing the pope. After the Council of Trent in the sixteenth century, when Pope Sixtus V (1585–90) reorganized the curia, a relatively large proportion of attention and resources had to be directed to the papal states: of the fifteen new curial departments, nine concerned the church and six governed the papal states.[69]

From the late seventeenth through the early twentieth centuries, the papacy's hold on the papal states was lost, regained, limited, and threatened, most dramatically by Napoleon and then the Italian unification movement called the *Risorgimento*. Around 1860, Italy took over the papal states, with Rome itself falling a decade later. For almost sixty years, the popes neither left Rome nor recognized the Italian state, living as the prisoners of the Vatican. In 1929, the Lateran Treaty was signed between the Italian Fascist dictator Benito Mussolini and Pope Pius XI (1922–39). This agreement established Vatican City as an independent state, albeit a tiny one: less than a quarter of a square mile and with just about a thousand inhabitants. With the papacy relieved of the papal states—a terribly heavy burden that had historically weighed the papacy down not only with financial and military worries, but more importantly with the trappings of worldliness, temporal power, and political entanglements—the popes were, in a sense, liberated. Conventional wisdom among church historians says that this liberation from the papal states permitted the twentieth-century popes to become the "oracles of God" and to take an unprecedented position of moral authority on the world stage personified dramatically during the pontificate of John Paul II (1978-2005).[70]

84. When did the Vatican become the papal headquarters?

The term *the Lateran* was used to refer to the Roman palace, church, and offices of the pope well into the Middle Ages. Pope Nicholas V in the middle of the fifteenth century relocated the center of papal business to the Vatican area of the city, in part because of the practical fact that he moved his own residence to an updated network of buildings there. After the Italian unification movement in the middle of the nineteenth century made the pope the prisoner of the Vatican, the papacy and the Vatican became almost synonymous. But this is only recent history; the fuller story reaches further back.

The original Lateran's connection with Christianity started when the Roman emperor Constantine gave his wife's palace, which had roots even earlier in Roman history to a family with the name Laterani, to the bishop of Rome early in the fourth century. This Lateran palace, whose main hall was called a basilica, was refurbished and seemed to function as both a church and a residence for the bishop of Rome. This church, or rather the several churches that stood there throughout the centuries as the buildings were in turn destroyed during invasion or burned down, came to be known as St. John Lateran, dedicated first to John the Baptist in the tenth century and then to John the evangelist in the twelfth century. The current basilica, with a facade dating to the eighteenth century, sits on the site of that original Roman Lateran palace. It is this church and not St. Peter's Basilica that is actually the pope's church in his role as bishop of the diocese of Rome.

Most people, of course, connect St. Peter's and not St. John Lateran with the Vatican. Both areas, the Lateran and the Vatican, are linked with the bishop of Rome from early in the church's life, but the Vatican holds a higher place of honor. Peter was almost surely killed and buried in the region known in the Roman Empire as the Vatican hill, which was not one of the seven traditional hills that comprised the sprawl that made up the ancient city of Rome. The Vatican hill was an outlying area, which was why it had become a place for mass graves. This was the same place where the Romans built a "circus": an open area used for races, games— and martyrdoms. The Roman emperor Nero especially enjoyed the circus and it was during his reign (54–68) that Peter and Paul were probably executed.

Peter's gravesite was venerated on this Vatican hill from the end of the first century and was excavated in the 1940s. Today it sits directly under the main altar of St. Peter's Basilica as part of an ancient necropolis or city of the dead, but this St. Peter's Basilica is not the original church. As part of the imperial protection of Christianity, Constantine had also ordered that a basilica be built at the site of Peter's tomb in addition to the Lateran center. Successive popes added to this church complex, building around the Vatican hill and then surrounding it with a protective wall by the ninth century. Medieval popes built progressively larger palaces and administrative areas to accommodate the growing bureaucracy of the papal monarchy and to house the officials who made it work, including the cardinals who lived in Rome most of the time.

As the popes' fortunes ebbed and flowed, so too did the decoration and upkeep of this first St. Peter's, which was in bad shape by the fourteenth century because the popes spent most of that century in Avignon. People began to talk in the fifteenth century about rebuilding. The current St. Peter's Basilica went up in stages: Nicholas V (1447–55) made the decision to build a new basilica and Julius II laid the foundation stone in 1506. But it wasn't until the reign of Sixtus V (1585–90) that the dome was completed, although decorating would continue for several decades more, and, in a sense, the painting and sculptures have never quite stopped. In the nearly two hundred years between idea and reality, the building proceeded hesitantly through alternating periods of frenzy and near total neglect, with some of the biggest names in the Renaissance contributing to the art and architecture. Raising money for the building involved all of Christian Europe and beyond, and it led to the kind of indulgence peddling that made Martin Luther criticize the church so vehemently, because some of the money raised from false relics was supposed to support the new basilica.

85. I'm confused when I hear *the Vatican, the Holy See,* and *Vatican City.* Are they all the same thing?

No. *The Vatican* is the most generic of these three terms. When most people say or think of the Vatican, they think of an official place of business or authority, along the lines of what people mean when they say "the White House said today…" or "Buckingham Palace officials told reporters…." As we've seen, the Vatican didn't become *the Vatican* in this sense until the Middle Ages and the Renaissance. The four medieval general councils held at Rome under direct papal supervision did not meet on the Vatican hill, for instance, but at the Lateran basilica and are called Lateran I, II, III, and IV. Not until the nineteenth century was a general council called by the name Vatican: Vatican I met in 1869–70 and Vatican II followed about a century later, 1962–65.

The Holy See is a more formal, diplomatic, and governmental title; the phrase is, in fact, the one used at the United Nations. Holy See—coming from the word *sedes* or chair/seat of authority—refers to the papacy's authority to rule the church, in a sense, and is often used interchangeably with *Apostolic See.* There is a unique character to the Holy See, because it does not have to refer to any geographic spot on the map. It is not the same thing as *Vatican City,* which is a geographic designation you will find in an atlas. Vatican

City is that city-state formed by the 1929 Lateran Treaty. It houses the papal apartments, St. Peter's Basilica, the Vatican Museum, gardens, residences, offices, bank, post office, electric plant, security, and legal system.[71]

86. How does such a large organization work?

You may be surprised to learn that an institution with about one billion members has a headquarters called the curia with less than three thousand staffers on site at the home office in Rome. The Vatican's main administrative office is called the Secretariat of State; the Secretary of State is something like a prime minister, though we must be sure to reiterate that this is not an elected post and there is no assistant or vice pope, which is how the secretary is sometimes inaccurately described. Think of him more as a chief operating officer. The Secretariat of State has two halves: one for internal church affairs and the other for relations with other nations and governments. Under this main office are a series of offices, generically called dicasteries, with some being of greater weight and influence than others. There are congregations (with some decision-making power), councils (more like advisory boards), tribunals (the legal system), and other administrative offices, although they have not always been organized this way. For the first thousand years of her life, the church was run by a mostly informal administrative curia that grew to be a bit more systematic during the medieval development of a papal monarchy. In 1588, Pope Sixtus V ordered the first major reorganization of the curia; his system stood without much adaptation until the 1917 *Code of Canon Law* trimmed some bureaucratic fat.

Popes can, on their own authority, reorganize the curia as they see fit. In 1967, as part of the atmosphere for reform ushered in by Vatican II, Paul VI made the curia more responsive to local matters. He brought in bishops from outside Rome to staff some offices and made sure diocesan bishops had regular input. He also tried to mix the staffing to make the Vatican more global. In 2006, Pope Benedict XVI decided one president would serve two offices, the

Pontifical Council for Culture and the Pontifical Council for Interreligious Dialogue, signaling his belief that the church's interests in interreligious dialogue and diverse cultures are served best when these two offices work more closely together. But the next year he restored a separate president for Interreligious Dialogue.

87. I heard that popes were slave owners and helped the slave trade. Is this true?

There were slaves in papal territories and early popes, including Gregory I (590–604), seemed to have accepted the ancient world's belief that slavery was part of the natural order, dating back to Aristotle's fourth century BC statement that some are born to rule and others to be ruled. During the early years of European exploration in the fifteenth century, first along the African coast and then progressively across the Atlantic, popes implicitly approved that non-Christians could be taken as slaves. Nicholas V allowed the Portuguese to do so in Africa in 1452 and 1455, while Alexander VI permitted the same for the Spanish in the New World in 1493. In 1488, Innocent VIII received and shared with his cardinals about a hundred Muslim slaves from Ferdinand of Aragon. As late as the early nineteenth century, Muslim slaves pulled the oars on the papal galleys. These are the facts, conditioned by their times to be sure, but they remain disturbing.

There is, on the other hand, a longer and stronger tradition of popes leading the fight against slavery. John VIII (872–82) declared slavery a sin and by the end of the first millennium, antiquity's acceptance of slavery, at least of Christians as slaves, had almost entirely disappeared in Europe. By the time Thomas Aquinas discussed slavery in the thirteenth century, it was commonly held to be a sin. In 1435, as the Spanish were enslaving the population of the Canary Islands off northwest Africa, Eugene IV gave slave owners fifteen days to free their slaves or face excommunication. Pius II called slavery a great crime in 1462. In 1537, Paul III issued three statements against slavery, stressing that the indigenous people of the New World were human beings who could accept Christianity and receive the sacraments, which were ideas that were not generally accepted by royal authorities and certainly not by slave traders and owners. Paul III noted that native peoples should be free even if they did not accept Christianity and repeated Eugene IV's threat of excommunication to slave owners. In 1639, Urban VIII reiterated the threat of excommunication. Benedict XIV in 1741, Gregory XVI in 1839, and Leo XIII in 1888 all condemned slavery, as well.

The fact that popes had to repeat their condemnations indicates the persistence of slavery and a certain lack of practical power on the papacy's part during these early modern centuries when secular governments distanced themselves from religious ties. Certainly Protestants like the British and Dutch with colonies in the Americas, Indies, Asia, and Africa would not heed papal condemnations. But the papacy's moral leadership persisted and was capped in 1992 by John Paul II. While visiting a slave prison off the coast of Senegal where Africans were held before being sent across the Atlantic, he confessed that baptized Christians had been slave traders and owners, acting in a manner completely against Christianity, and asked God for forgiveness.[72]

E. Symbolism

88. The pope wears a lot of symbolic vestments and jewelry. What do they all mean?

Most of the papal vestments and jewelry are common to all bishops, but with some variations given the pope's unique position. The pope wears a pointed hat with two short slips of cloth running down the back called a miter, which is one of the symbols of his role as a bishop. It dates back to the last few centuries of the first millennium and seems to have originated in Rome, then spread to other areas. You might see paintings of bishops and saints before the year 1000 wearing a miter, but these are anachronistic representations, artistic license if you will, where a medieval or Renaissance painter read back into ancient times something that was common in his own period. Underneath the miter is the zucchetto; a bishop's is purple or violet, a cardinal's is scarlet red, but only the pope's is white.

Also, and again like all bishops, the pope wears a ring; in the pope's case, it is known as the fisherman's ring, inscribed with an image of St. Peter in a fishing boat. He holds a staff called a crozier to represent his role as shepherd of his flock. Some bishops use a simple shepherd's crook: this was favored by the late archbishop of New York, Cardinal John O'Connor, for instance, because he said it reminded him of what his job was. Other croziers are more elaborate. Both John Paul II and Benedict XVI often selected a staff topped not by a crook but by a crucifix. The pope also wears around his neck a cross on a long chain that is often pinned up close to the center of his chest; it is called a pectoral cross from the Latin word *pectus,* for breast or chest (think: pectoral muscles). Once more, all bishops wear this cross at all times, although when a bishop is in a black suit—something the pope never wears—this pectoral cross is typically tucked into his inside jacket pocket as a practical matter so it doesn't bang into anything as he moves about.

The pope wears a pallium around his neck. A pallium is a circular piece of white wool about three inches wide marked by six black silk crosses, four of which are decorated with pins, with two slips of wool a bit over a foot long hanging down the front and back. A metropolitan archbishop's pallium symbolizes his jurisdiction over a geographic area, while the pope's pallium represents the universal jurisdiction as Peter's successor that is his alone. Pope Benedict XVI wears an elaborate form of the pallium: a version larger and longer than the usual one that looks like a stole tossed over the left shoulder, with red crosses instead of black. This style was used in the ancient church: mosaics depict early bishops wearing such a pallium, although it often looks like the decoration on their vestment instead.

89. Didn't popes wear something called a triple crown?

Yes. In fact, there have been several triple crowns over the centuries. Medieval engravings, paintings, and sculptures show what looks like a metallic cone with three small crowns or tiaras of progressively smaller circumferences working their way bottom to top. Other depictions, and even the crowns themselves, are of a somewhat inverted cone, with the smallest crown at the bottom and two more, each slightly wider, working their way to the top. Several triple crowns still exist; one that belonged to Pius IX in the nineteenth century now sits in the Basilica of the Sacred Heart at the University of Notre Dame in South Bend, Indiana. There is an official triple crown in the Vatican today. Each year on June 29, the feast day of Saints Peter and Paul, it is placed on the head of the statue of St. Peter in his basilica in Rome.

This triple crown (alternately called a tiara or the triregnum) evolved over the centuries, starting with the introduction of a miter, perhaps with a single crown ringing the base to symbolize the pope's authority over the papal states, a bit before the year 1000. As the Middle Ages progressed, two more tiers or crowns were added, perhaps by Boniface VIII and Clement V in the late thirteenth and early fourteenth century or Benedict XII in the middle of the fourteenth century. The additions were probably intended to indicate that the pope's spiritual and moral authority were ultimately higher than any temporal authority. The three crowns were frequently elaborate and studded with jewels, then topped by an orb representing the globe and a cross. The crowns were likely designed in imitation of—or competition with—royal crowns because the papacy was building a monarchy at this time to compete with France, England, and other secular powers.

These three crowns have been interpreted in various ways. A liturgical book from 1596 identifies the three powers this way: the pope is father of princes and kings, rector or governor of the world, and vicar of Christ on earth. Another interpretation identi-

fies the pope's role as universal shepherd or bishop over other bishops, his jurisdictional supremacy, and his temporal power over the
papal states. Still another interpretation, this one ringing with
high-minded theology, says the three crowns stand for the pope's
authority over the church on earth (the church militant), over
believers who are penitent or pilgrims on their way to God (perhaps meaning purgatory or the church suffering), and even in partnership with God in heaven (the church triumphant). A far more
spiritual, benign, and pastoral explanation identifies the three
crowns with the pope's roles as priest, pastor, and teacher. This last
interpretation is the one linked most closely with his ordination as
a bishop.

Popes no longer wear the triple crown. Paul VI in 1963 was
the last one to be crowned at a coronation; his was a gift from the
people of Milan, whom he served as archbishop before his election
to the papacy. (Milan had done the same in 1922 for Pius XI, who
also had been archbishop of Milan before his election.) Paul VI
then abolished the use of the triple crown. Many accounts say that
he sold it and gave the money to the poor, but the fate of that particular triple crown remains in question.

Neither John Paul I nor John Paul II used the triple crown in
1978; John Paul I was the first pope to be invested with the pallium only, instead. Because a pope is no longer crowned, the ceremony at which he ceremoniously takes office is no longer called a
coronation. Instead, we say that a pope is installed or celebrates an
inaugural Mass, but this means his first public Mass as pope, not an
inauguration in the sense of an American president taking the oath
of office. An American president has no authority until that
moment, while the new pope has been pope with full power from
the moment he accepted his election in the conclave. Benedict
XVI also did not use the triple crown and he went a step further
by removing it from his coat of arms.

90. Why does each pope get his own coat of arms?

A coat of arms is a throwback to the medieval age of heraldry when great families used these pictorial and symbolic devices to describe their power, their origins, and above all, their identities. Bishops, cardinals, and popes have long had coats of arms, starting with Pope Innocent III (1198–1216). Their designs vary greatly. John Paul II's for instance, was about as simple as a coat of arms can be: a field colored blue, the traditional color for the Virgin Mary, and a large M, also for Mary, under a cross. All papal coats of arms display the crossed keys of St. Peter, one gold and the other silver, from Matthew 16:19; the crossed keys have also, at least in the past, been used to describe the pope's temporal and spiritual power. The triple crown and the keys also appear on Vatican City's flag and seal as well as on the coat of arms for the Holy See and Vatican City. Until Pope Benedict XVI, all papal coats of arms had the triple crown, too, but Benedict substituted a miter at the top and a pallium at the bottom. This miter has three bands across its face and the Vatican Web site explains that they "recall the symbolism of the tiara."

91. Whatever happened to that chair to carry popes around St. Peter's?

That chair was called a *sedia gestatoria*. It's an Italian phrase indicating a portable papal throne: a chair mounted on a platform with hoops through which are inserted sturdy poles for men to heave onto their shoulders. Sometimes a canopy was added over the chair and often the procession was accompanied by the waving of white-feathered fans. Popes weren't the only people to use such a chair. We find early accounts of emperors, especially in the Byzantine Empire, being carried around. In addition, Roman emperors and lesser officials, medieval kings and lords, and royal and rich people throughout the centuries were often transported in a sedan chair, though this was typically more like a closed carriage and carried closer to the ground.

Like the papal tiara, the chair fell out of use as part of Vatican II's atmosphere of toning down the pomp and circumstance. While using it smacked of triumphalism—the pope carried around like a conquering hero, especially because it was employed more commonly after the Protestant challenges of the sixteenth century—the chair had a very practical purpose. Before wide-screen concert and television screens, the sedia gestatoria was a tool to raise the pope above everyone else so the audience could see him. It was last used by John Paul I, who only agreed to climb aboard after Vatican officials convinced him that he couldn't otherwise be seen. When you look at the matter this way, a bullet-proof popemobile is simply a next-generation version of a movable throne that is useful and sensible.

92. Why does the new pope change his name?

In many cultures, a change of name indicates a change in status or stage of life; in the Hebrew Scripture, for example, Abram and Sarai became Abraham and Sarah when God established his covenant (Gen 17). The papal tradition of taking a new name fits into this kind of ritual, but it is not directly related to it. The historical truth is far less prosaic. When a man named Mercury was elected pope in 533, he didn't think it was a good idea for the bishop of Rome to share a name with a pagan Roman god, so he became John II (533–35). Most, though not all, of the following popes continued the tradition of taking a new name to symbolize the new office so that within a few centuries it was common to do so. The last man to keep his own name was Marcello Cervini, who became Marcellus II (1555).

93. When did popes start wearing white?

You'll get different answers depending on whom you ask because several religious orders wear a white cassock or habit and want to take the credit. Without getting involved in any ecclesiastical turf battles or bragging rights, it's safe to say that most historians point to Innocent V (1276) as the first pope to wear white. His reason was probably very straightforward: he was a Dominican and he simply continued to wear the same white habit as pope that he had worn as a friar. Not every pope after him wore white, however, but after another Dominican pope, Pius V (1566–72) did so, white became the pope's color.

PART III
Papal Potpourri[1]

94. Was there really a Pope Joan?

No, there was not a Pope Joan, but why the legend of the popess has lasted is itself an interesting story.[2]

First, let's look at the legend, which has no basis in fact: none of the facts, names, dates, and places fit into the historical record. According to the stories, which began in the thirteenth century, at some point in the centuries before that an intelligent and literate woman had disguised herself as a man, began a career as a scribe, and over time achieved a number of successively higher church positions, including cardinal and then pope. After several years, this pope was discovered to be a woman when she delivered a child as she climbed into a horse's saddle or while riding in procession between St. Peter's and the Lateran. In various versions of the story, a crowd that witnessed the event pulled her down to beat her, tied her to the horse's tail, or stoned her to death. So common was the story that learned Italian humanists like Petrarch and Boccaccio in the fourteenth century mentioned her; a sculpture of a Pope Joan was even placed alongside other popes in a Siena cathedral around that time.

Second, let's look at why the legend lasted. One group of people might use it to try to prove that a woman should not be a priest, let alone the pope, while others employ the legend to make the opposite point: a woman's smarts are what count and if she can do the job, she should be able to. It may be that the legend was a way of representing the fact that some powerful Roman women had played a major role in selecting popes around the turn of the first millennium. Other legends grew out of it, especially the false notion that medieval popes had to sit on a chair with a hole in it—something like an elaborate chamberpot—so they could be inspected and proven to be male. As you can imagine, the legend of Pope Joan became a popular rallying point for Protestant critics and Catholic defenders in the sixteenth and following centuries,

145

although it was ironically a French Protestant who categorically refuted the legend in the seventeenth century. As with so much of what we have been discussing in this book, it is important to separate fact from fiction, to understand why the fictions persist, and to learn from informed history and not rumor or hearsay.

95. Who were the youngest and oldest popes?

The youngest pope was John XII, elected at the age of 18, who reigned 955–64. He was a notorious pope in a notorious time. John was the illegitimate son of Rome's civil leader, who engineered his son's succession as prince and election as pope even though there was a pope still alive and regulations prohibited the naming of a successor in the current pope's lifetime. John, intrigued with powerful rulers, was deposed and replaced by one of them, returned himself to power and challenged his own successor, and then, in accordance with the stories that said he treated the Lateran like a brothel, supposedly died of a stroke suffered while sleeping with a married woman.

The oldest man elected pope may have also been the oldest man to serve as pope. Celestine III (1191–98) was eighty-five when elected; he died at ninety-three. (We are not sure about his date of birth, however; we are sure about the birth and death dates for Leo XIII, who died at almost ninety-three-and-a-half years old in 1903.) Celestine had middling success in protecting the church from a powerful and ambitious Holy Roman Emperor named Henry VI, but he was able to continue building, reorganizing, and administering the papal monarchy fairly efficiently, with special attention to canon law and financial matters. Celestine was so worn out that he suggested to the college of cardinals he might abdicate, but only if they agreed to elect his handpicked successor. The cardinals refused; Celestine stayed on but died just a few weeks after this discussion, and his choice for successor lost to another candidate.

96. Which popes had the longest and shortest reigns?

Tradition has it that Peter reigned thirty-five years, but the historical record is not precise. Still, this period of thirty-five years was known as St. Peter's years, and it was believed that no pope would ever surpass that span of time. So far, no one has.

Excluding Peter, then, the longest reigning pope was Pius IX, who reigned for slightly more than thirty-one-and-a-half years (1846–78). To put that timespan into perspective, he was elected pope fifteen years before the American Civil War began and he died thirteen years after it ended, at the age of eighty-five. The next longest papacy was that of John Paul II, who reigned a bit longer than twenty-six-and-a-half years (1978–2005). He passed Leo XIII (1878–1903), who was pope just shy of twenty-five-and-a-half years. Taken together, the reigns of Pius IX and Leo XIII combined for the longest period with the fewest popes: fifty-seven years (1846–1903) with just two popes.

There have been a number of very short reigns. Many people assumed the sudden death of John Paul I in 1978 after just over a month in office marked the shortest papacy in history. This is not true: the shortest papacy belongs to Urban VII, who died after twelve days in office in 1590. Celestine IV follows: his papacy lasted seventeen days in 1241. Beyond that, there have been eighteen reigns of two months or less, with the most recent (before John Paul I) being Leo XI, who was pope for twenty-six days in 1605.

97. Is it true that some popes were married and had children?

Yes, throughout history we find popes who were married—including Peter, whose mother-in-law was healed by Jesus—and had children. Celibacy as the absolute and enforced norm may have been on the books in the first millennium, but it was not always followed until about the eleventh century, when popes began to crack down on priests with children, not least because priests were handing down their profession, church property, and sacred vessels and vestments in something of an apprenticeship or family business operation. During the Renaissance, men who openly had mistresses and children were elected pope, though it is hard to prove that they fathered children while pope.

98. Were there any papal father-son combinations?

Yes, there were at least three that we know of. Anastasius I (399–401) and Innocent I (401–17), a fairly strong and impressive pair, are the only combination to succeed each other without anyone in between their reigns. Then there was Hormisdas (514–23) and Silverius (536–37), with five men in between during a time of particularly high confusion and turnover. Next is Sergius III (904–911) and his illegitimate son John XI (931–35 or 936), who had been named pope through the behind-the-scenes efforts of his mother, Sergius III's mistress. Her name was Marozia and, for all intents and purposes, she ran Rome.

99. People are already calling John Paul II "the Great." Where does that title come from and how many "Greats" have there been already?

You will most often hear that there were two "Greats," but this is a mistake: there have been three. The two everyone mentions are Leo I (440–61) and Gregory I (590–604). The third, mostly unknown Great is Nicholas I (858–67).

It's not clear why these three popes were called Great. Some believe it's because they turned back barbarian invaders from Rome, but only Leo I did this. It's more likely that they were recognized as Great because they defended papal authority on several fronts: from the East (Leo I and Nicholas I), from imperial incursion (Leo I and Nicholas I), and from within (Leo I, Gregory I, and Nicholas I). Gregory, in addition, was known not only as a skilled administrator, but as a pope who took his roles as pastor and evangelist quite seriously.

The phrase *the Great*, which comes from the Latin *magnus,* is not a formal or legal title but rather one that has been bestowed on popes by Christians who commonly believed they stood above the crowd. This is the sense contemporary people have about John Paul II, so it may well be that if they start calling him the Great, the phrase will stick.

100. How many popes are saints?

The church has had more than 260 popes, eighty-one of whom have been declared saints, which works out to a little less than a third. Tradition says that all but one of the first forty-eight, including Peter and ending just shy of the year 500, are saints.[3] Another thirty popes were recognized as saints in the following centuries, concluding this period of papal saints with Gregory VII, who died in 1085. These numbers date from a time when people were declared saints by acclamation: everyone just understood and declared publicly that a person was holy. This process is not unlike how those three popes came to be called Great and was essentially repeated at John Paul II's funeral in 2005. Crowds held up signs and shouted "Santo subito!" ("A saint right away!"). When a television news anchor asked me when John Paul II would be declared a saint, I responded: "We may have just seen it." As with Mother Teresa, Vatican paperwork will probably catch up with a sainted reality everyone already acknowledges.

Since canonization developed during the Middle Ages as a formal process of inquiry, examination, and declaration of sanctity under papal supervision, there have been three papal saints: Celestine V (1294, who was elected and resigned within a five-month period), Pius V (1566–72), and Pius X (1903–14).[4]

Epilogue

101. The story of the papacy is inspiring, but there have been lots of flawed popes. Do you think people might have their faith weakened or lose heart by studying the entire picture of the papacy?

For years, I've told my students, readers, and public audiences a simple fact: if you want to save your faith, study church history. Given all that's happened, the Holy Spirit must be in charge. I acknowledge here that I'm speaking more as a practicing Catholic than as a church historian, but even secular historians I know often say that a higher authority must be in charge because it always seems that when the church is in trouble, someone, usually someone unexpected, steps forward to handle the crisis in an innovative way. I've heard many people say that the very facts of the church's survival, renewal, and even flourishing must be proof that she is of divine origin and receiving heavenly help, because the papacy has not collapsed under the weight of human frailty. These facts are a reminder that we must always view the story of the papacy as operating, at the same time, in both the city of God as well as in the city of mankind.

Appendix: List of Popes (and Antipopes)

The following list is based primarily on the Vatican's official *Annuario Pontificio,* a kind of annual directory or statistical year-book, but amended from other sources.[1] Acknowledged antipopes are indented and in italics. Note that the numbering of popes can be confusing and imprecise, because the numbers assigned to antipopes have not always been valid.[2]

Peter (d. ca. 64)
Linus (ca. 66–76)
Anacletus (ca. 79–91)
Clement (ca. 91–100)
Evaristus (ca. 100–109)
Alexander I (ca. 109–16)
Sixtus I (ca. 116–25)
Telesphorus (ca. 125–36)
Hyginus (ca. 138–42)
Pius I (ca. 142–55)
Anicetus (ca. 155–66)
Soter (ca. 166–74)
Eleutherius (ca. 174–89)
Victor I (ca. 189–98)
Zephyrinus (ca. 199–217)
Callistus I (ca. 217–22)
   Hippolytus (ca. 217–35)
Urban I (ca. 222–30)
Pontian (230–35)
Anterus (235–36)

Fabian (236–50)
Cornelius (251–53)
   Novatian (251–58)
Lucius I (253–54)
Stephen I (254–57)
Sixtus II (257–58)
Dionysius (260–68)
Felix I (269–74)
Eutychian (275–83)
Gaius (283–96)
Marcellinus (ca. 296–304)
Marcellus I (306–8)
Eusebius (310)
Miltiades (311–14)
Sylvester I (314–35)
Mark (336)
Julius I (337–52)
Liberius (352–66)
   Felix II (355–65)
Damasus I (366–84)

Ursinus (366–67)
Siricius (384–99)
Anastasius I (399–401)
Innocent I (401–17)
Zosimus (417–418)
Eulalius (418–419)
Boniface I (418–22)
Celestine I (422–32)
Sixtus III (432–40)
Leo I (440–61)
Hilary (461–68)
Simplicius (468–83)
Felix III (II) (483–92)
Gelasius I (492–96)
Anastasius II (496–98)
Symmachus (498–514)
Lawrence (498–99,
501–6)
Hormisdas (514–23)
John I (523–26)
Felix IV (III) (526–30)
Boniface II (530–32)
Dioscorus (530)
John II (533–35)
Agapitus I (535–36)
Silverius (536–37)
Vigilius (537–55)
Pelagius I (556–61)
John III (561–74)
Benedict I (575–79)
Pelagius II (579–90)
Gregory I (590–604)
Sabinian (604–6)
Boniface III (607)
Boniface IV (608–15)

Adeodatus (Deusdedit) I
(615–18)
Boniface V (619–25)
Honorius I (625–38)
Severinus (640)
John IV (640–42)
Theodore I (642–49)
Martin I (649–53)
Eugene I (654–57)
Vitalian (657–72)
Adeodatus (Deusdedit) II
(672–76)
Donus (676–78)
Agatho (678–81)
Leo II (682–83)
Benedict II (684–85)
John V (685–86)
Conon (686–87)
Theodore (687)
Paschal (687)
Sergius I (687–701)
John VI (701–5)
John VII (705–7)
Sisinnius (708)
Constantine (708–15)
Gregory II (715–31)
Gregory III (731–41)
Zacharias (741–52)
Stephen II (752–57)
Paul I (757–67)
Constantine (767–68)
Philip (768)
Stephen III (768–72)
Hadrian I (772–95)
Leo III (795–816)

Stephen IV (816–17)
Paschal I (817–24)
Eugene II (824–27)
Valentine (827)
Gregory IV (827–44)
John (844)
Sergius II (844–47)
Leo IV (847–55)
Benedict III (855–58)
Anastasius Bibliothecarius (855)
Nicholas I (858–67)
Hadrian II (867–72)
John VIII (872–82)
Marinus I (882–84)
Hadrian III (884–85)
Stephen V (885–91)
Formosus (891–96)
Boniface VI (896)
Stephen VI (896–97)
Romanus (897)
Theodore II (897)
John IX (898–900)
Benedict IV (900–903)
Leo V (903)
Christopher (903–4)
Sergius III (904–11)
Anastasius III (911–13)
Lando (913–14)
John X (914–28)
Leo VI (928)
Stephen VII (928–31)
John XI (931–35 or 936)
Leo VII (936–39)
Stephen VIII (939–42)
Marinus II (942–46)

Agapitus II (946–55)
John XII (955–64)
Leo VIII (963–65)
Benedict V (964–66)
John XIII (965–72)
Benedict VI (973–74)
Boniface VII (974, 984–85)
Benedict VII (974–83)
John XIV (983–84)
John XV (985–96)
Gregory V (996–99)
John XVI (997–98)
Sylvester II (999–1003)
John XVII (1003)
John XVIII (1004–9)
Sergius IV (1009–12)
Benedict VIII (1012–24)
Gregory VI (1012)
John XIX (1024–32)
Benedict IX (1032–44, 1045, 1047–48)
Sylvester III (1045)
Gregory VI (1045–46)
Clement II (1046–47)
Damasus II (1048)
Leo IX (1049–54)
Victor II (1055–57)
Stephen IX (1057–58)
Benedict X (1058–59)
Nicholas II (1059–61)
Alexander II (1061–73)
Honorius II (1061–64)
Gregory VII (1073–85)
Clement III (1080, 1084–1100)

Victor III (1086–87)
Urban II (1088–99)
Paschal II (1099–1118)
   Theodoric (1100–1101)
   Albert (1101)
   Sylvester IV (1105–11)
Gelasius II (1118–19)
   Gregory VIII (1118–21)
Callistus II (1119–24)
   Celestine II (1124)
Honorius II (1124–30)
Innocent II (1130–43)
   Anacletus II (1130–38)
   Victor IV (1138)
Celestine II (1143–44)
Lucius II (1144–45)
Eugene III (1145–53)
Anastasius IV (1153–54)
Hadrian IV (1154–59)
Alexander III (1159–81)
   Victor IV (1159–64)
   Paschal III (1164–68)
   Callistus III (1168–78)
   Innocent III (1179–80)
Lucius III (1181–85)
Urban III (1185–87)
Gregory VIII (1187)
Clement III (1187–91)
Celestine III (1191–98)
Innocent III (1198–1216)
Honorius III (1216–27)
Gregory IX (1227–41)
Celestine IV (1241)
Innocent IV (1243–54)
Alexander IV (1254–61)

Urban IV (1261–64)
Clement IV (1265–68)
Gregory X (1271–76)
Innocent V (1276)
Hadrian V (1276)
John XXI (1276–77)
Nicholas III (1277–80)
Martin IV (1281–85)
Honorius IV (1285–87)
Nicholas IV (1288–92)
Celestine V (1294)
Boniface VIII (1294–1303)
Benedict XI (1303–4)
Clement V (1305–14)
John XXII (1316–34)
   Nicholas V (1328–30)
Benedict XII (1335–42)
Clement VI (1342–52)
Innocent VI (1352–62)
Urban V (1362–70)
Gregory XI (1370–78)
Urban VI (1378–89)
Boniface IX (1389–1404)
Innocent VII (1404–6)
Gregory XII (1406–15)
  Avignon line:
    Clement VII (1378–94)
    Benedict XIII (1394–1417)
    Clement VIII (1423–29)
    Benedict XIV (1425–?)
  Pisan/conciliar line:
    Alexander V (1409–10)
    John XXIII (1410–15)
Martin V (1417–31)
Eugene IV (1431–47)

Felix V (1440–49)
Nicholas V (1447–55)
Callistus III (1455–58)
Pius II (1458–64)
Paul II (1464–71)
Sixtus IV (1471–84)
Innocent VIII (1484–92)
Alexander VI (1492–1503)
Pius III (1503)
Julius II (1503–13)
Leo X (1513–21)
Hadrian VI (1522–23)
Clement VII (1523–34)
Paul III (1534–49)
Julius III (1550–55)
Marcellus II (1555)
Paul IV (1555–59)
Pius IV (1559–65)
Pius V (1566–72)
Gregory XIII (1572–85)
Sixtus V (1585–90)
Urban VII (1590)
Gregory XIV (1590–91)
Innocent IX (1591)
Clement VIII (1592–1605)
Leo XI (1605)
Paul V (1605–21)
Gregory XV (1621–23)
Urban VIII (1623–44)
Innocent X (1644–55)

Alexander VII (1655–67)
Clement IX (1667–69)
Clement X (1670–76)
Innocent XI (1676–89)
Alexander VIII (1689–91)
Innocent XII (1691–1700)
Clement XI (1700–1721)
Innocent XIII (1721–24)
Benedict XIII (1724–30)
Clement XII (1730–40)
Benedict XIV (1740–58)
Clement XIII (1758–69)
Clement XIV (1769–74)
Pius VI (1775–99)
Pius VII (1800–1823)
Leo XII (1823–29)
Pius VIII (1829–30)
Gregory XVI (1831–46)
Pius IX (1846–78)
Leo XIII (1878–1903)
Pius X (1903–14)
Benedict XV (1914–22)
Pius XI (1922–39)
Pius XII (1939–58)
John XXIII (1958–63)
Paul VI (1963–78)
John Paul I (1978)
John Paul II (1978–2005)
Benedict XVI (2005–)

Notes

Prologue

1. Raymond E. Brown, *An Introduction to the New Testament* (New York: Doubleday, 1997), 279.

2. An insightful study of the scriptural basis of this topic from an ecumenical perspective is found in Raymond E. Brown, et al., eds., *Peter in the New Testament* (London: Geoffrey Chapman, 1973).

Part I

1. Some of this material in part I echoes a book where I previously discussed these developments. See Christopher M. Bellitto, *Ten Ways the Church Has Changed* (Boston: Pauline Books & Media, 2006), 53–78. On this early period, I am indebted generally to W.H.C. Frend, *The Rise of Christianity* (Philadelphia: Fortress Press, 1984). For many details of papal lives and actions throughout this Part, I have relied on J.N.D. Kelly, *The Oxford Dictionary of Popes* (Oxford: Oxford University Press, 1986).

2. Origen, *Commentary on Matthew,* 12.10, 14.

3. Tertullian, *Prescription Against Heretics,* 32; Irenaeus, *Against Heresies,* 3.2–4.

4. As translated in Henry Bettenson, ed., *Documents of the Christian Church,* 2nd ed. (London: Oxford University Press, 1967), 80–81.

5. Bettenson, *Documents of the Christian Church,* 79.

6. Bettenson, *Documents of the Christian Church,* 81.

7. For a complete discussion and many examples, see Charles Odahl, "God and Constantine: Divine Sanction for Imperial Rule in the First Christian Emperor's Early Letters and Art," *Catholic Historical Review* 81 (1995): 327–52.

8. Bettenson, *Documents of the Christian Church*, 22–23; Frend, *The Rise of Christianity*, 626-29, 727–28.

9. Gerhart B. Ladner, *The Idea of Reform: Its Impact on Christian Thought and Action in the Age of the Fathers* (Cambridge, MA: Harvard University Press, 1959), 300.

10. For these and other examples, see especially Leo I's *Sermons* 3–5, 82, and his *Letters* 14, 25.

11. Brian Tierney, *The Crisis of Church and State 1050–1300* (Toronto: University of Toronto Press, 1988), 9.

12. Tierney, *The Crisis of Church and State,* 13–14.

13. Eamon Duffy, *Saints and Sinners: A History of the Popes* (New Haven: Yale University Press, 1997), 87.

14. An older, but still relevant and helpful, discussion of this papal ideology (vestments, personnel, court and chancery systems, and oaths of allegiance) is found in Walter Ullmann, *The Growth of Papal Government in the Middle Ages* (London: Methuen, 1955), 310–43.

15. An interesting book that explores in detail just how much the Gregorian popes transformed the papacy, let alone the legal and administrative structures in secular monarchies that were influenced by these papal developments, is Harold J. Berman, *Law and Revolution: The Formation of the Western Legal Tradition* (Cambridge, MA: Harvard University Press, 1983), especially 85–269. See also I.S. Robinson, *The Papacy, 1073–1198: Continuity and Innovation* (Cambridge: Cambridge University Press, 1990) and Colin Morris, *The Papal Monarchy: The Western Church from 1050 to 1250* (Oxford: Clarendon Press, 1989).

16. See Duffy, *Saints and Sinners,* 215. In 1829, there were 646 dioceses in the world; of these, bishops of 555 were appointed by the state, although not always unilaterally. For centuries, for instance, leading priests of a diocese would nominate a man for bishop and the state would mostly accede to their wishes, only sometimes after consultation with papal authorities. It was not until the 1917 *Code of Canon Law* that the church actually stated, legally and explicitly,

that only the pope can name bishops in the West; he confirms or accepts the nominations of bishops in Eastern rites.

17. For the references to Gregory's letters, see Ephraim Emerton, trans., *The Correspondence of Pope Gregory VII: Selected Letters from the Registrum* (New York: Columbia University Press, 1990).

18. As noted in Maureen C. Miller, *Power and the Holy in the Age of the Investiture Conflict: A Brief History with Documents* (Boston: Bedford/St. Martin's, 2005), 81, followed by the twenty-seven propositions. This slim volume is a handy introduction to the many contexts and layers of conflict and meaning embodied in the papal-imperial power struggle.

19. Emerton, *The Correspondence of Pope Gregory VII*, 15, 26–27, 54, 121–22, 153.

20. Emerton, *The Correspondence of Pope Gregory VII*, 149.

21. Emerton, *The Correspondence of Pope Gregory VII*, 86–91; Tierney, *The Crisis of Church and State*, 57–61.

22. Emerton, *The Correspondence of Pope Gregory VII*, 166–75; Tierney, *The Crisis of Church and State*, 66–73.

23. Duffy, *Saints and Sinners*, 101.

24. For the entire story, see Henry Chadwick, *East and West: The Making of a Rift in the Church* (Oxford: Oxford University Press, 2003).

25. As quoted in Aristeides Papadakis, *The Christian East and the Rise of the Papacy. The Church 1071–1453 AD* (Crestwood, NY: St. Vladimir's Seminary Press, 1994), 158, 165.

26. Tierney, *The Crisis of Church and State*, 188–89.

27. For a fair assessment of the Avignon years that judiciously weighs the evidence, see G. Mollat, *The Popes at Avignon*, 9th ed., trans. Janet Love (New York: Harper and Row, 1965).

28. As quoted in *Readings in Western Civilization*, vol. 4, *Medieval Europe*, eds. Julius Kirshner and Karl F. Morrison (Chicago: The University of Chicago Press, 1986), 424–25.

29. There was no provision in canon law, then or now, that said an election made in fear was invalid, which makes quite plausible the Roman claim to an uninterrupted chain from Peter even-

tually through Urban VI and beyond. The best account of the events and legal issues involved remains Walter Ullmann, *Origins of the Great Schism* (London: Methuen, 1948). Current church law states that even if a papal election is bought and the man elected pope is guilty of simony (the buying or selling of a church office), the election is still valid and the man remains the legitimate pope.

30. For the best presentation of conciliarism's orthodox roots, see Brian Tierney, *Foundations of the Conciliar Theory: The Contribution of the Medieval Canonists from Gratian to the Great Schism* (Leiden: Brill, 1998). This is an enlarged edition of his classic study, first published in 1955 by Cambridge University Press. The introduction to the new edition takes up much of the scholarship of the intervening decades.

31. For a summary of the councils mentioned in this and the next several questions, see Christopher M. Bellitto, *The General Councils: A History of the Church's Twenty-One Church Councils from Nicaea to Vatican II* (Mahwah, NJ: Paulist Press, 2002).

32. John "XXIII" is correct: since he was later deposed, his number didn't count, leaving the way for Cardinal Angelo Roncalli to choose "John" in 1958, even though this dark history had made the name unattractive for about 550 years. There was further confusion as to Roncalli's number because there had been no John XX due to a counting error.

33. C.M.D. Crowder, ed., *Unity, Heresy and Reform, 1378–1460. The Conciliar Response to the Great Western Schism* (New York: St. Martin's Press, 1977), 83.

34. For an insightful and lively discussion of conciliarism's history at and since the Middle Ages, essential reading is Francis Oakley, *The Conciliarist Tradition: Constitutionalism in the Catholic Church 1300–1870* (Oxford: Oxford University Press, 2003).

35. Norman Tanner, ed. *Decrees of the Ecumenical Councils*, 2 vols. (London: Sheed & Ward, 1990), 1:514–20, 529–34.

36. Crowder, *Unity, Heresy and Reform,* 179–81. It wasn't unusual for conciliarists to cross over to the papalist side as the tide turned throughout the fifteenth century. For an interesting discus-

sion of the transformation of one such humanist, see Thomas M. Izbicki, Gerald Christianson, and Philip Krey, trans., *Reject Aeneas, Accept Pius: Selected Letters of Aeneas Sylvius Piccolomini (Pope Pius II)* (Washington, DC: The Catholic University of America Press, 2006).

37. Scott H. Hendrix, *Luther and the Papacy: Stages in a Reformation Conflict* (Philadelphia: Fortress Press, 1981), 124–25.

38. There are many translations; this excerpt is taken from Lewis W. Spitz, ed. *The Protestant Reformation,* 3rd ed. (Needham Heights, MA: Ginn Press, 1990), 56–58.

39. At the end of his life, Luther published *Against the Papacy at Rome, Founded by the Devil,* again with woodcuts depicting the pope in diabolical and apocalyptic terms for those who could not read. In the nineteenth-century United States, Catholics (derisively called Romanists or papists since the time of Luther) were seen as instruments of Antichrist among evangelicals. For some examples and context, see William M. Shea, *The Lion and the Lamb. Evangelicals and Catholics in America* (Oxford: Oxford University Press, 2004), especially 111, 126–27, 342 n. 45. For a more comprehensive view of this Antichrist rhetoric and occasional application to the papacy, see Bernard McGinn, *Antichrist: Two Thousand Years of the Human Fascination with Evil* (San Francisco: HarperSanFrancisco, 1994).

40. "Adrian VI's Instruction to Chieregati, 1522," in John C. Olin, ed., *The Catholic Reformation: Savonarola to Ignatius Loyola* (New York: Fordham University Press, 1992), 125.

41. "The *Consilium de emendanda ecclesia 1537,*" in John C. Olin, ed., *Catholic Reform: From Cardinal Ximenes to the Council of Trent 1495–1563* (New York: Fordham University Press, 1990), 78.

42. Robert Bellarmine, *De potestate summi pontificis,* ch. 31.

43. For a primer on what Trent actually was and did, see John W. O'Malley, "The Council of Trent: Myths, Misunderstandings, and Misinformation," in *Spirit, Style, Story: Essays Honoring John W. Padberg, S.J.,* ed. Thomas M. Lucas (Chicago: Loyola Press, 2002), 205–26.

44. On this debate, see the comprehensive treatment and proposal in John W. O'Malley, *Trent and All That: Renaming Catholicism in the Early Modern Era* (Cambridge, MA: Harvard

University Press, 2000). Some of the seminal historiography is gathered in David M. Luebke, ed., *The Counter-Reformation* (Oxford: Basil Blackwell, 1999).

45. Giuseppe Alberigo, "From the Council of Trent to 'Tridentinism'," translated by Emily Michelson, in *From Trent to Vatican II: Historical and Theological Investigations,* eds. Raymond F. Bulman and Frederick J. Parrella (Oxford: Oxford University Press, 2006), 19–37; William V. Hudon, "The Papacy in the Age of Reform, 1513–1644," in *Early Modern Catholicism,* eds. Kathleen M. Comerford and Hilmar M. Pabel (Toronto: University of Toronto Press, 2001), 46–66.

46. For more complete treatment, see Owen Chadwick, *The Popes and European Revolution* (Oxford: Clarendon Press, 1981) and *A History of the Popes, 1830–1914* (Oxford: Clarendon Press, 1998).

47. R. Po-Chia Hsia, *The World of Catholic Renewal 1540–1770* (Cambridge: Cambridge University Press, 1998), 92–95.

48. Chadwick, *The Popes and European Revolution,* 76–77.

49. As quoted in Klaus Schatz, *Papal Primacy From Its Origins to the Present,* trans. John A. Otto and Linda M. Maloney (Collegeville, MN: The Liturgical Press, 1996), 188.

50. In all fairness to Joseph II, however, the Austrian church was indeed in need of many reforms that he successfully accomplished where popes had failed or not even tried: Chadwick, *The Popes and European Revolution,* 412–17.

51. Schatz, *Papal Primacy,* 140–43.

52. Duffy, *Saints and Sinners,* 204.

53. The story of the papacy's seventeenth century stumbles and eighteenth century recovery is told succinctly and well by Sheridan Gilley, "The Emergence of the Modern Papacy: 1721–1878," in Paul Johnson, *The Papacy,* ed. Michael Walsh (London: Weidenfeld & Nicolson, 1977), 166–87.

54. Gregory XVI, *Mirari vos,* in *The Papal Encyclicals 1740–1878,* ed. Claudia Carlen (Raleigh, NC: McGrath Publishing Company, 1981). Throughout, this encyclical implicitly and explicitly condemns aspects of liberalism and the idea that the church

should embrace modernity, but for a prime statement, see no. 10 (237).

55. A representative anthology of modernist writings is Bernard M.G. Reardon, ed., *Roman Catholic Modernism* (Stanford: Stanford University Press, 1970). For a fuller account, see Marvin R. O'Connell, *Critics on Trial: An Introduction to the Modernist Crisis* (Washington, DC: Catholic University of America Press, 1994).

56. John Cornwell, *Hitler's Pope: The Secret History of Pius XII* (New York: Viking, 1999). For a similar approach, see Susan Zuccotti, *Under His Very Windows: The Vatican and the Holocaust in Italy* (New Haven: Yale University Press, 2000). Title words like plot, secret, or conspiracy feed on a reading public poised to believe in the existence of a dark and hidden church history, conditioned especially in recent years by the fictional *Da Vinci Code* and the all-too-real clergy sexual abuse and cover-up revelations.

57. An excellent, dispassionate introduction to the debate is by José M. Sánchez, *Pius XII and the Holocaust: Understanding the Controversy* (Washington, DC: Catholic University of America Press, 2001). Sánchez has won praise for fairly examining the charges against Pius XII leveled by some scholars, some journalists, and certain sectors of the general public by laying them alongside historical records and contexts. He looks at the motives of those defending and attacking Pius XII. See also John T. Pawlikowski, "The Vatican and the Holocaust: Unresolved Issues," in *Jewish-Christian Encounters Over the Centuries: Symbiosis, Prejudice, Holocaust, Dialogue,* eds. Marvin Perry and Frederick M. Schweitzer (New York: Peter Lang, 1994), 293–312; Eugene Fisher, "Annotated Bibliography of Recent Works on Pope Pius XII," *Catholic International* (May 2002): 87–93; and David G. Dalin, *The Myth of Hitler's Pope: How Pope Pius XII Rescued Jews from the Nazis* (Washington, DC: Regnery, 2005).

Part II

1. John Paul II, *Ut unum sint*, no. 96; official translation as it appears on the Vatican Web site, www.vatican.va. For a summary

and assessment of this encyclical, see Edward Idris Cassidy, *Ecumenism and Interreligious Dialogue: Unitatis Redintegratio, Nostra Aetate* (New York/Mahwah, NJ: Paulist Press, 2005), 30–43.

2. An informative survey is Klaus Schatz, *Papal Primacy From Its Origins to the Present,* trans. John A. Otto and Linda M. Maloney (Collegeville, MN: The Liturgical Press, 1996).

3. The statements are found in Joseph A. Burgess and Jeffrey Gros, eds., *Building Unity: Ecumenical Dialogues with Roman Catholic Participation in the United States* (Mahwah, NJ: Paulist Press, 1989), 125–59 with this quotation on 137. Background essays are in P.C. Empie, T. Austin, and J.A. Burgess, eds., *Papal Primacy and the Universal Church* (Minneapolis: Augsburg, 1974). More recent material and discussions are treated in Adriano Garuti, *Primacy of the Bishop of Rome and Ecumenical Dialogue* (San Francisco: Ignatius Press, 2004) and Walter Kasper, ed., *The Petrine Ministry: Catholics and Orthodox in Dialogue* (Mahwah, NJ: The Newman Press, 2006). For discussions on this topic within the Anglican-Roman Catholic International Commission (ARCIC), see its 1999 statement, "The Gift of Authority," which invited Anglicans to accept universal primacy and Catholics to accept greater collegiality. The text is available at http://www.prounione.urbe.it/dia-int/arcic/doc/e_arcicII_05.html.

4. See, for instance, the bold but balanced response to John Paul II's invitation by John R. Quinn, *The Reform of the Papacy: The Costly Call to Christian Unity* (New York: Crossroad, 1999).

5. Translated from Italian in *Annuario Pontificio 2006* (Vatican City: Libreria Editrice Vaticana, 2006), 23.

6. For more on this topic, see a source that informs this section at several points: Richard R. Gaillardetz, *The Church in the Making: Lumen Gentium, Christus Dominus, Orientalium Ecclesiarum* (New York/Mahwah, NJ: Paulist Press, 2006), 32–36, 77–80, 123–27, 179–81.

7. *Lumen gentium,* nos. 21–23 and "Preliminary Note of Explanation"; official translation as it appears on the Vatican Web site, www.vatican.va.

8. *Code of Canon Law,* c. 336; official translation as it appears on the Vatican Web site, www.vatican.va.

9. *Code of Canon Law,* cc. 331, 333; official translation as it appears on the Vatican Web site, www.vatican.va.

10. John Paul II, *Ut unum sint,* nos. 94–95; official translation as it appears on the Vatican Web site, www.vatican.va.

11. For background, see Thomas Reese, ed., *Episcopal Conferences: Historical, Canonical and Theological Studies* (Washington, DC: Georgetown University Press, 1989).

12. Regional councils are essentially nonexistent today, having been replaced by episcopal conferences and national synods of bishops. At least one commentator believes strongly that the loss of regional conferences, so vital in the church's earlier life, is quite lamentable—"one of the gravest wounds in Christian history"—because they represented a place where a broad range of matters was discussed openly. See Norman Tanner, *Was the Church Too Democratic? Councils, Collegiality and the Church's Future* (Bangalore, India: Dharmaram Publications, 2003), 14–25.

13. Avery Dulles, "From Ratzinger to Benedict," *First Things* (February 2006): 24–29, traces the much-discussed development of Ratzinger's theological stances from his early years as a Vatican II *peritus,* who was quite open to episcopal collegiality and local authority, to his more centralized conception of papal authority.

14. Gaillardetz, *The Church in the Making,* 127–32.

15. For a survey, see Christopher M. Bellitto, *The General Councils: A History of the Twenty-One Church Councils Nicaea to Vatican II* (New York/Mahwah, NJ: Paulist Press, 2002).

16. *Code of Canon Law,* cc. 337–341; official translation as it appears on the Vatican Web site, www.vatican.va. See also *Lumen gentium,* no. 22.

17. For a complete discussion of this issue, see Jane E. Merdinger, *Rome and the African Church in the Time of Augustine* (New Haven: Yale University Press, 1997), which informs this and the next question.

18. Cyprian, *Sententiae Episcoporum, Patrologia Latina,* vol. 3, col. 1054. A side-by-side comparison and translation of Cyprian's original and revised statements on the subject may be found in Maurice Bévenot, trans. and ed., *De Ecclesiae Catholicae Unitate* (Oxford: Clarendon Press, 1971), 63–64. See also Henry Bettenson, ed., *Documents of the Christian Church,* 2nd ed. (London: Oxford University Press, 1967), 71–74. In the sixteenth century, John Calvin was attracted to Cyprian for his revised interpretation of episcopal equality and solidarity: G.S.M. Walker, *The Churchmanship of St. Cyprian* (Richmond, VA: John Knox Press, 1969), 68. The story of the fight between Stephen and Cyprian is summarized, with their sharp language intact, in W.H.C. Frend, *The Rise of Christianity* (Philadelphia: Fortress Press, 1984), 351–57. The best biographical treatment of Cyprian and especially this point remains Peter Hinchcliff, *Cyprian of Carthage and the Unity of the Catholic Church* (London: Geoffrey Chapman Publishers, 1974).

19. Bettenson, *Documents of the Christian Church,* 81–82.

20. For a summary, see Gaillardetz, *The Church in the Making,* 80–82, 132–33. A remarkably public and amicable exchange of ideas on the related topic of the relationship between the universal church and local churches occurred between Joseph Ratzinger and Walter Kasper, who discussed and critiqued each other's thoughts in both scholarly and popular publications. For an introduction and discussion of this exchange, with full citations, see Killian McDonnell, "The Ratzinger/Kasper Debate: The Universal Church and Local Churches," *Theological Studies* 63 (2002): 227–50.

21. Frend, *The Rise of Christianity,* 678.

22. Norman P. Tanner, ed., *Decrees of the Ecumenical Councils,* 2 vols. (London: Sheed & Ward/Washington, DC: Georgetown University Press, 1990), 2:815–16. For help understanding the issues and terms, see Richard R. Gaillardetz, *Teaching with Authority: A Theology of the Magisterium in the Church* (Collegeville, MN: The Liturgical Press, 1997), 104–8, 147–57.

23. Francis A. Sullivan, *Creative Fidelity: Weighing and Interpreting Documents of the Magisterium* (New York/Mahwah, NJ: Paulist Press,

1996), 53. For a discussion of as many as a dozen prior statements that seem to meet the criteria, see Sullivan, *Creative Fidelity*, 80–92.

24. John Paul II, *Ordinatio sacerdotalis*, no. 4; official translation as it appears on the Vatican Web site, www.vatican.va. For a fuller treatment of the issues, see Richard R. Gaillardetz, "Infallibility and the Ordination of Women," *Louvain Studies* 21 (1996): 3–24. For brief discussions respectfully doubting the infallibility of this statement, see Sullivan, *Creative Fidelity*, 181–84, and Bernard Prusak, *The Church Unfinished: Ecclesiology Through the Centuries* (New York/Mahwah, NJ: Paulist Press, 2004), 340. Although neither Sullivan nor Prusak use the expression "creeping infallibility," this phrase has been raised, often quietly, in theological circles to object to what some considered attempts during John Paul II's papacy to wrap a broad range of papal statements in a mantle of infallibility without invoking the *ex cathedra* formula.

25. *Lumen gentium,* no. 25; official translation as it appears on the Vatican Web site, www.vatican.va. The issues of extraordinary and ordinary magisterium, and the related levels of definitive and nondefinitive teaching (among other categories), are complex and related to this discussion, but they would pull us too far afield. A very helpful explanation, with useful schematics, is provided by Gaillardetz, *Teaching with Authority;* a distillation by the same author is *By What Authority? A Primer on Scripture, the Magisterium and the Sense of the Faithful* (Collegeville, MN: The Liturgical Press, 2003). For a full discussion of *Lumen gentium* no. 25 and the infallibility of the ordinary universal magisterium, see Richard R. Gaillardetz, *Witnesses to the Faith: Community, Infallibility, and the Ordinary Magisterium of Bishops* (New York: Paulist Press, 1992).

26. Maureen C. Miller, *Power and the Holy in the Age of the Investiture Conflict: A Brief History with Documents* (Boston: Bedford/ St. Martin's, 2005), 82.

27. See, in general, Brian Tierney, *Origins of the Papal Infallibility, 1150–1350: A Study on the Concepts of Infallibility, Sovereignty, and Tradition in the Middle Ages* (Leiden: E. J. Brill, 1972).

28. Schatz, *Papal Primacy*, 117–23.

29. Tanner, *Decrees of the Ecumenical Councils,* 2:805.

30. Roger Aubert, *Le pontificat de Pie IX (1846–1878),* vol. 21 of *Histoire de l'Église depuis les origines jusqu'à nos jours,* eds. Augustin Fliche and Victor Martin (Paris: Bloud et Gay, 1962), 303; Eamon Duffy, *Saints and Sinners: A History of the Popes* (New Haven: Yale University Press, 1997), 230.

31. Tanner, *Decrees of the Ecumenical Councils,* 2:815–16.

32. Owen Chadwick, *A History of the Popes 1830–1914* (Oxford: Clarendon Press, 1998), 210–11. The question of tradition is related to the idea of *magisterium:* how doctrines develop is as important as who decides what is authentic development and what are correct statement of those doctrines. In addition to the classic study by Yves M.-J. Congar, *Tradition and Traditions,* trans. Michael Naseby and Thomas Rainborough (New York: Macmillan, 1967), see Thomas P. Rausch, *The Roots of the Catholic Tradition* (Wilmington, DE: Michael Glazier, 1986) and, more recently, Terrence W. Tilley, *Inventing Catholic Tradition* (Maryknoll, NY: Orbis Books, 2000), and John E. Thiel, *Senses of Tradition: Continuity and Development in Catholic Faith* (Oxford: Oxford University Press, 2000).

33. Tanner, *Decrees of the Ecumenical Councils,* 1:125–26, 161–62.

34. For the pope's homily and the prayers themselves, see *The Pope Speaks* 45:4 (July/August 2000): 242–48.

35. A sketchy collection of these statements, though incomplete because it was published before the end of John Paul II's papacy, is by Luigi Accattoli, *When a Pope Asks Forgiveness: The Mea Culpa's of John Paul II,* trans. Jordan Aumann (Boston: Pauline Books & Media, 1998).

36. John Paul II, *Tertio millennio adveniente,* no. 33; official translation as it appears on the Vatican Web site, www.vatican.va.

37. *Origins* 29 (16 March 2000): 625–44.

38. For discussions that both praise and critique the apologies and explanations, see Christopher M. Bellitto, "Teaching the Church's Mistakes: Historical Hermeneutics in *Memory and Reconciliation: The Church and the Faults of the Past,*" and Bernard P.

Prusak, "Theological Considerations—Hermeneutical, Ecclesiological, Eschatological—Regarding *Memory and Reconciliation: The Church and the Faults of the Past,"* both in *Horizons: The Journal of the College Theology Society* 32 (2005), 123–35 and 136–51, respectively, with footnotes there indicating sources of the wider scholarly conversation.

39. Most histories of the papacy and/or conclaves of necessity treat the history of the college of cardinals. Apart from such general treatment, a dated though enjoyable resource is Glenn D. Kittler, *The Papal Princes: A History of the Sacred College of Cardinals* (New York: Funk and Wagnalls, 1960).

40. The key study is Stephan Kuttner, *"Cardinalis:* The History of a Canonical Concept," *Traditio* 3 (1945): 129–214.

41. It is often observed that new cardinals from rich archdioceses are assigned Roman titular churches in need of repair. Cardinal Francis Spellman, archbishop of New York (1939–67), for example, undertook a major excavation and renovation of his titular Church of Saints John and Paul. The work was paid for, in large part, by the Kennedy family, whom Spellman knew from his native Boston.

42. There is a similar contemporary example. A priest might have been born, trained, and ordained in a different country from the one in which he currently lives; through a formal process, he is accepted into his new diocese and is canonically (or legally) transferred from the authority of his original bishop to his new diocese's bishop.

43. As translated by the Vatican Information Service, 20 February 2001.

44. It may be that monks adopted this practice because a fully or partially shaved head was an indication of slave status in the late Roman Empire. The tonsure therefore indicated that the monk was choosing to live for a master, in this case God.

45. Today's academic processions at college graduations bring these outfits back to life, with the new graduates wearing stiff mor-

tarboards and the professors sporting softer doctoral caps. These caps, or berets, are probably the source of the biretta.

46. Bishops have purple or violet versions of both the zucchetto and the biretta; the pope wears a white zucchetto but no biretta.

47. The Vatican Web site, www.vatican.va, regularly updates the composition of the college of cardinals by number, age, and geographic distribution.

48. For historical comparison and developments, see John F. Broderick, "The Sacred College of Cardinals: Size and Geographical Composition (1099–1986)," *Archivum historiae pontificiae* 25 (1987): 7–71.

49. *Code of Canon Law*, c. 351; official translation as it appears on the Vatican Web site, www.vatican.va.

50. As the papacy of John Paul II drew to its obvious and inevitable conclusion in the late 1990s and first few years of the twenty-first century, a number of studies (and novels) concerning papal conclaves appeared, naturally of widely varying quality. Among the better of these volumes, see John L. Allen's readable and journalistic *Conclave* (New York: Image Doubleday, 2002) as well as Frederic J. Baumgartner's more scholarly and complete *Behind Locked Doors: A History of the Papal Elections* (New York: Palgrave Macmillan, 2003).

51. Paul VI, *Romano Pontifici Eligendo*, 1 October 1975, no. 42.

52. Peter Hebblethwaite, *The Year of Three Popes* (Cleveland: William Collins, Inc., 1979), 72.

53. John Paul II, *Universi Dominici Gregis*, 22 February 1996, preface.

54. Lawrence Elliott, *I Will Be Called John* (New York: Dutton, 1973), 248. Another version of the story has John XXIII declaring, "Everyone wanted me to become pope except the tailors." See Albert J. Nevins, *The Story of Pope John XXIII* (New York: Grosset and Dunlap, 1966), 8.

55. Hebblethwaite, *The Year of Three Popes*, 77.

56. Baumgartner, *Behind Locked Doors*, 13–16.

57. We shall soon see that Lyons II in 1274 formalized the conclave. It is interesting to note that the canons of this general council that follow the rules for a papal conclave deal with other church elections, making the link of fair and free elections between the church's head and her body. Tanner, *Decrees of the Ecumenical Councils,* 1:314–22.

58. Baumgartner, *Behind Locked Doors,* 202, 209–10.

59. An excellent resource, on which I have relied in this section on conclaves, is by Frederic J. Baumgartner, " 'I Will Observe Absolute and Perpetual Secrecy':The Historical Background of the Rigid Secrecy Found in Papal Elections," *Catholic Historical Review* 89 (2003): 165–81.

60. Baumgartner, *Behind Locked Doors,* 202–3.

61. Baumgartner, *Behind Locked Doors,* 241–45.

62. A summary of the issues was offered by James H. Provost, "What If the Pope Became Disabled?" *America* (30 September 2000): 7–9.

63. *Canto* III: 1–60. It is generally, though not universally, agreed that Dante is referring to Celestine V in this passage. This spot at hell's doorstep is reserved for those who lived without praise or blame. *Canto* XXVII: 87–105 has a more specific reference to Celestine V by Boniface VIII, his successor (called "the prince of the new Pharisees" by Dante), who says that "my predecessor" did not prize the papal keys. About a decade after Celestine's resignation in 1294, Dante probably started working on the *Inferno,* which is the first of the three parts of his *Comedy,* followed by *Purgatorio* and *Paradiso.* A critic of papal worldliness at a time when it was a growing problem, Dante placed a handful of popes in hell with Celestine.

64. Duffy, *Saints and Sinners,* 83. At this same point, Duffy describes what could be called character assassination and metaphoric deposition.This event is the infamous "cadaver synod" of 897, when Stephen VI propped the decaying body of his predecessor Formosus (891–96) on a chair and put him on trial. Stephen found him guilty of perjury, then had his blessing fingers

chopped off and the body thrown into the Tiber. As noted, an element of poetic justice followed when Stephen was deposed and strangled.

65. Peter Hebblethwaite, *Paul VI. The First Modern Pope* (Mahwah, NJ: Paulist Press, 1993), 568–69.

66. This answer is informed by John L. Allen, Jr., *All the Pope's Men: The Inside Story of How the Vatican Really Works* (New York: Doubleday, 2004), 78–83.

67. For these and other similar selections, see John D. Anderson and Elizabeth T. Kennan, trans., *Five Books on Consideration: Advice to a Pope* (Kalamazoo, MI: Cistercian Publications, 1976), 42–45, 56–61, 110–18.

68. Erasmus's *Praise of Folly* treats the papacy in sections 57–61. This translation is taken from John P. Dolan, trans., *The Essential Erasmus* (New York: The New American Library, 1964), 156–58.

69. Robert Bireley, *The Refashioning of Catholicism, 1450–1700* (Washington, DC: The Catholic University of America Press, 1999), 63.

70. The phrase is from Duffy, *Saints and Sinners,* 245.

71. For further details on this answer and the next, see Allen, *All the Pope's Men,* 23–45.

72. The careful reader will note a variety of points of view in the following resources that inform this answer: John T. Noonan, Jr., *A Church That Can and Cannot Change: The Development of Catholic Moral Teaching* (Notre Dame, IN: University of Notre Dame Press, 2005), 17–123; Rodney Stark, *The Victory of Reason* (New York: Random House, 2005), 28–31, 200–202; Rodney Stark, *For the Glory of God: How Monotheism Led to Reformations, Science, Witch-Hunts, and the End of Slavery* (Princeton: Princeton University Press, 2003), 329–37; Joel S. Panzer, *The Popes and Slavery* (New York: Alba House, 1996), which contains appendices with papal and other church statements denouncing slavery.

Part III

1. Trivia buffs will want to explore Nino Lo Bello, *The Incredible Book of Vatican Facts and Papal Curiosities: A Treasury of Trivia* (New York: Gramercy Books, 2002). A more sober and shorter treatment of some of the same topics is found in a list of papal "firsts" and "lasts" in Richard P. McBrien, *Lives of the Popes* (New York: HarperSanFrancisco, 1997), 453–57.

2. The legend is so widespread that the author of the leading handbook of popes included an appendix on Pope Joan, which informs this section: J.N.D. Kelly, *The Oxford Dictionary of Popes* (Oxford: Oxford University Press, 1986), 331–32. A very interesting and responsible survey of the story, its history, and the uses to which the legend has been placed and why is provided by Alain Boureau, *The Myth of Pope Joan,* trans. Lydia G. Cochrane (Chicago: The University of Chicago Press, 2001).

3. The only one of these first popes not called a saint is Liberius (352–66), who tried to hold out against pressure to reject the Nicene creed, but caved in a bit and agreed to condemn Athanasius, the champion of Nicaea I (325), who explained how Jesus was "one in being with the Father." Liberius eventually righted himself, but his was a troubled reign.

4. For a history of canonization, see Kenneth L. Woodward, *Making Saints: How the Catholic Church Determines Who Becomes a Saint, Who Doesn't, and Why* (New York: Touchstone, 1996); the statistics in this paragraph are found on 281–82.

Appendix

1. *Annuario Pontificio 2006* (Vatican City: Libreria Editrice Vaticana, 2006), 7–20; J.N.D. Kelly, *The Oxford Dictionary of Popes* (Oxford: Oxford University Press, 1986), 1–4; Eamon Duffy, *Saints and Sinners: A History of the Popes* (New Haven: Yale University Press, 1997), 293-99.

2. The most confusing numbering relates to the name John. The confusion begins with a counting error dating to the tumul-

tuous ninth through eleventh centuries, when there were many Johns but not, in fact, a John XX. The next pope to take the name John, in 1276, was incorrectly reckoned as XXI. An already muddled picture grew worse when a John XXIII was deposed and subsequently assigned antipope status in 1415.

For Further Reading

There is a deluge of books on the market, some of them old standards that still hold up well, others simply instant books that are written too quickly or updated slightly around the time of a papal transition. To list even a small percentage would take several pages. Because the task is enormous, I have decided to go in the other direction and select just a few volumes—the best of the bunch—that I find authoritative, reliable, judicious, and well grounded. What follows are suggestions, some of which exist already in this book's notes (where recommended articles are also listed, though omitted here), that will allow the reader to explore particular periods, topics, or approaches to the papacy. These are the volumes to which I often turn; their own texts, notes, and bibliographies may guide you further, too.

General

Eamon Duffy. *Saints and Sinners: A History of the Popes.* Third Edition. New Haven: Yale/Nota Bene, 2006.
J.N.D. Kelly and Michael Walsh. *The Oxford Dictionary of Popes.* Updated Edition. Oxford: Oxford University Press, 2006.
John W. O'Malley, ed. *The Papacy: An Encyclopedia.* 3 vols. New York/London: Routledge, 2002.

The Vatican

John L. Allen, Jr. *All the Pope's Men: The Inside Story of How the Vatican Really Works.* New York: Doubleday, 2004.
Frank J. Coppa, ed. *Encyclopedia of the Vatican and Papacy.* Westport, CT: Greenwood Press, 1999.

Particular periods (in approximate chronological order)

Robert B. Eno. *The Rise of the Papacy*. Wilmington, DE: Michael Glazier, 1990.

Jane E. Merdinger. *Rome and the African Church in the Time of Augustine*. New Haven: Yale University Press, 1997.

Bernhard Schimmelpfennig. *The Papacy*. Translated by James Sievert. New York: Columbia University Press, 1992.

Colin Morris. *The Papal Monarchy: The Western Church from 1050 to 1250*. Oxford: Clarendon Press, 1989.

I.S. Robinson. *The Papacy, 1073–1198: Continuity and Innovation*. Cambridge: Cambridge University Press, 1990.

Aristeides Papadakis. *The Christian East and the Rise of the Papacy. The Church 1071–1453 AD*. Crestwood, NY: St. Vladimir's Seminary Press, 1994.

G. Mollat. *The Popes at Avignon*. Ninth Edition. Translated by Janet Love. New York: Harper and Row, 1965.

Walter Ullmann. *Origins of the Great Schism*. London: Methuen, 1948.

Scott H. Hendrix. *Luther and the Papacy: Stages in a Reformation Conflict*. Philadelphia: Fortress Press, 1981.

A. D. Wright. *Early Modern Papacy: From the Council of Trent to the French Revolution, 1564–1789*. New York: Longman, 2000.

Owen Chadwick. *The Popes and European Revolution*. Oxford: Clarendon Press, 1981.

————. *A History of the Popes, 1830–1914*. Oxford: Clarendon Press, 1998.

Frank J. Coppa. *The Modern Papacy Since 1789*. New York: Longman, 1998.

Particular topics

Frederic J. Baumgartner. *Behind Locked Doors: A History of the Papal Elections*. New York: Palgrave Macmillan, 2003.

Henry Chadwick. *East and West: The Making of a Rift in the Church.* Oxford: Oxford University Press, 2003.

Francis Oakley. *The Conciliarist Tradition: Constitutionalism in the Catholic Church 1300–1870.* Oxford: Oxford University Press, 2003.

Klaus Schatz. *Papal Primacy From Its Origins to the Present.* Translated by John A. Otto and Linda M. Maloney. Collegeville, MN: The Liturgical Press, 1996.

Brian Tierney. *Origins of the Papal Infallibility, 1150–1350: A Study on the Concepts of Infallibility, Sovereignty, and Tradition in the Middle Ages.* Leiden: E. J. Brill, 1972.

Other Books
in This Series

101 QUESTIONS AND ANSWERS ON THE BIBLE
by Raymond E. Brown, SS

101 QUESTIONS AND ANSWERS ON THE BIBLICAL TORAH
by Roland E. Murphy, O Carm

101 QUESTIONS AND ANSWERS ON THE CHURCH
by Richard P. McBrien

101 QUESTIONS AND ANSWERS ON CONFUCIANISM,
DAOISM, AND SHINTO
by John Renard

101 QUESTIONS AND ANSWERS ON DEACONS
by William T. Ditewig

101 QUESTIONS AND ANSWERS ON ISLAM
by John Renard

101 QUESTIONS AND ANSWERS ON PAUL
by Ronald D. Witherup

101 QUESTIONS AND ANSWERS ON VATICAN II
by Maureen Sullivan, OP

101 QUESTIONS AND ANSWERS ON CATHOLIC MARRIAGE
PREPARATION
by Rebecca Nappi and Daniel Kendall, SJ

101 QUESTIONS AND ANSWERS ON THE FOUR LAST
THINGS
by Joseph T. Kelley

101 QUESTIONS AND ANSWERS ON THE EUCHARIST
by Giles Dimock, OP

101 QUESTIONS AND ANSWERS ON CATHOLIC
MARRIED LIFE
by Catherine Johnston; Daniel Kendall, SJ; and Rebecca Nappi

101 QUESTIONS AND ANSWERS ON SAINTS
by George P. Evans

Other Books
Under the Former Series Title

RESPONSES TO 101 QUESTIONS ON THE DEAD SEA
SCROLLS
by Joseph A. Fitzmyer, SJ

RESPONSES TO 101 QUESTIONS ABOUT JESUS
by Michael L. Cook, SJ

RESPONSES TO 101 QUESTIONS ON THE PSALMS
AND OTHER WRITINGS
by Roland E. Murphy, O Carm

RESPONSES TO 101 QUESTIONS ON DEATH AND
ETERNAL LIFE
by Peter C. Phan

RESPONSES TO 101 QUESTIONS ON HINDUISM
by John Renard

RESPONSES TO 101 QUESTIONS ON BUDDHISM
by John Renard

RESPONSES TO 101 QUESTIONS ON THE MASS
by Kevin W. Irwin

RESPONSES TO 101 QUESTIONS ON GOD AND EVOLUTION
by John F. Haught

RESPONSES TO 101 QUESTIONS ON
CATHOLIC SOCIAL TEACHING
by Kenneth R. Himes, OFM